Textbook Outlines, Highlights, and Practice Quizzes

Macroeconomics

by Michael Parkin, 12 Edition

All "Just the Facts101" Material Written or Prepared by Cram101 Textbook Reviews

Title Page

"Just the Facts101" is a Content Technologies publication and tool designed to give you all the facts from your textbooks. Register for the full practice test for each of your chapters for virtually any of your textbooks.

Facts101 has built custom study tools specific to your textbook. We provide all of the factual testable information and unlike traditional study guides, we will never send you back to your textbook for more information.

YOU WILL NEVER HAVE TO HIGHLIGHT A BOOK AGAIN!

Facts101 StudyGuides

All of the information in this StudyGuide is written specifically for your textbook. We include the key terms, places, people, and concepts... the information you can expect on your next exam!

Facts101

Only Facts101 gives you the outlines, highlights, and PRACTICE TESTS specific to your textbook. Facts101 sister Cram101.com is an online application where you'll discover study tools designed to make the most of your limited study time.

www.Cram101.com

Copyright © 2016 by Content Technologies, Inc. All rights reserved.

"FACTS101"®, "Cram101"® and "Never Highlight a Book Again!"® are registered trademarks of Content Technologies, Inc.

ISBN(s): 9781538827543. PUBI-6.20161119

STUDYING MADE EASY

This Cram101 notebook is designed to make studying easier and increase your comprehension of the textbook material. Instead of starting with a blank notebook and trying to write down everything discussed in class lectures, you can use this Cram101 textbook notebook and annotate your notes along with the lecture.

Our goal is to give you the best tools for success.

For a supreme understanding of the course, pair your notebook with our online tools at www.cram101.com

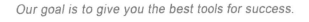

Our Online Access program is a simple way for us to keep our promise and provide you the best studying tools, regardless of where you purchased your Cram101 textbook notebook. As long as you let us know you are intereested in a free online access account we will set it up for you for 180 days.

Online Access:

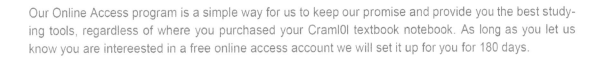

SIMPLE STEPS TO GET A FREE ACCOUNT:

Email Travis.Reese@cram101.com
Include:
Order number
ISBN of Guide
Retailer where purchased

Macroeconomics
Michael Parkin, 12

CONTENTS

1. What Is Economics? 5
2. The Economic Problem 15
3. Demand and Supply 23
4. Measuring GDP and Economic Growth 31
5. Monitoring Jobs and Inflation 43
6. Economic Growth 55
7. Finance, Saving, and Investment 63
8. Money, the Price Level, and Inflation 75
9. The Exchange Rate and the Balance of Payments 93
10. Aggregate Supply and Aggregate Demand 109
11. Expenditure Multipliers 121
12. The Business Cycle, Inflation, and Deflation 131
13. Fiscal Policy 141
14. Monetary Policy 154
15. International Trade Policy 167

1. What Is Economics?

CHAPTER OUTLINE: KEY TERMS, PEOPLE, PLACES, CONCEPTS

	Discouraged worker
	Depreciation
	Economics
	Incentive
	Macroeconomics
	Microeconomics
	Scarcity
	Factors of production
	Good
	Human capital
	Land
	Production
	Capital
	Entrepreneurship
	Financial capital
	Interest
	Profit
	Wage
	Efficiency
	Globalization
	Invisible hand

1. What Is Economics?
CHAPTER OUTLINE: KEY TERMS, PEOPLE, PLACES, CONCEPTS

	Bank
	Climate change
	Monopoly
	Mixed economies
	Opportunity cost
	Margin
	Marginal cost
	Economic model
	Normative statement
	Positive statement
	Causation
	Correlation
	Point
	Ceteris paribus
	Money

1. What Is Economics?

CHAPTER HIGHLIGHTS & NOTES: KEY TERMS, PEOPLE, PLACES, CONCEPTS

Discouraged worker	Not to be confused with Disgruntled worker. In economics, a discouraged worker is a person of legal employment age who is not actively seeking employment or who does not find employment after long-term unemployment. This is usually because an individual has given up looking or has had no success in finding a job, hence the term 'discouraged'.
Depreciation	In accountancy, depreciation refers to two aspects of the same concept:•the decrease in value of assets (fair value depreciation), and•the allocation of the cost of assets to periods in which the assets are used (depreciation with the matching principle). The former affects the balance sheet of a business or entity, and the latter affects the net income that they report. Generally the cost is allocated, as depreciation expense, among the periods in which the asset is expected to be used. This expense is recognized by businesses for financial reporting and tax purposes.
Economics	Economics is the social science that studies the behavior of individuals, households, and organizations, when they manage or use scarce resources, which have alternative uses, to achieve desired ends. Agents are assumed to act rationally, have multiple desirable ends in sight, limited resources to obtain these ends, a set of stable preferences, a definite overall guiding objective, and the capability of making a choice. There exists an economic problem, subject to study by economic science, when a decision (choice) has to be made by one or more resource-controlling players to attain the best possible outcome under bounded rational conditions.
Incentive	An incentive is something that motivates an individual to perform an action. The study of incentive structures is central to the study of all economic activities (both in terms of individual decision-making and in terms of co-operation and competition within a larger institutional structure). Economic analysis, then, of the differences between societies (and between different organizations within a society) largely amounts to characterizing the differences in incentive structures faced by individuals involved in these collective efforts.
Macroeconomics	Macroeconomics is a branch of economics dealing with the performance, structure, behavior, and decision-making of an economy as a whole, rather than individual markets. This includes national, regional, and global economies. With microeconomics, macroeconomics is one of the two most general fields in economics.
Microeconomics	Microeconomics is a branch of economics that studies the behavior of individuals and small impacting players in making decisions on the allocation of limited resources . Typically, it applies to markets where goods or services are bought and sold.

1. What Is Economics?

CHAPTER HIGHLIGHTS & NOTES: KEY TERMS, PEOPLE, PLACES, CONCEPTS

Scarcity	Scarcity is the fundamental economic problem of having seemingly unlimited human wants in a world of limited resources. It states that society has insufficient productive resources to fulfill all human wants and needs. Additionally, scarcity implies that not all of society's goals can be pursued at the same time; trade-offs are made of one good against others.
Factors of production	In economics, factors of production are the inputs to the production process. Finished goods are the output. Input determines the quantity of output i.e. output depends upon input.
Good	In economics, a good is a material that satisfies human wants and provides utility, for example, to a consumer making a purchase. A common distinction is made between 'goods' that are tangible property (also called goods) and services, which are non-physical. Commodities may be used as a synonym for economic goods but often refer to marketable raw materials and primary products.
Human capital	Human capital is the stock of competencies, knowledge, habits, social and personality attributes, including creativity, cognitive abilities, embodied in the ability to perform labor so as to produce economic value. It is an aggregate economic view of the human being acting within economies, which is an attempt to capture the social, biological, cultural and psychological complexity as they interact in explicit and/or economic transactions. Many theories explicitly connect investment in human capital development to education, and the role of human capital in economic development, productivity growth, and innovation has frequently been cited as a justification for government subsidies for education and job skills training.
Land	In economics, land comprises all naturally occurring resources whose supply is inherently fixed. Examples are any and all particular geographical locations, mineral deposits, and even geostationary orbit locations and portions of the electromagnetic spectrum. Natural resources are fundamental to the production of all goods, including capital goods.
Production	Production is a process of combining various material inputs and immaterial inputs in order to make something for consumption (the output). It is the act of creating output, a good or service which has value and contributes to the utility of individuals. Economic well-being is created in a production process, meaning all economic activities that aim directly or indirectly to satisfy human needs.
Capital	In economics, capital goods, real capital, or capital assets are already-produced durable goods or any non-financial asset that is used in production of goods or services. Capital goods are not significantly consumed in the production process though they may depreciate. How a capital good or is maintained or returned to its pre-production state varies with the type of capital involved.
Entrepreneurship	In political economics, entrepreneurship is the process of identifying and starting a business venture, sourcing and organizing the required resources and taking both the risks and rewards associated with the venture.

1. What Is Economics?

CHAPTER HIGHLIGHTS & NOTES: KEY TERMS, PEOPLE, PLACES, CONCEPTS

Financial capital	Financial capital is any economic resource measured in terms of money used by entrepreneurs and businesses to buy what they need to make their products or to provide their services to the sector of the economy upon which their operation is based, i.e. retail, corporate, investment banking, etc.
Interest	Interest is a fee paid by a borrower of assets to the owner as a form of compensation for the use of the assets. It is most commonly the price paid for the use of borrowed money, or money earned by deposited funds. When money is borrowed, interest is typically paid to the lender as a percentage of the principal, the amount owed to the lender.
Profit	In neoclassical microeconomic theory, the term profit has two related but distinct meanings. Economic profit is similar to accounting profit but smaller because it reflects the total opportunity costs (both explicit and implicit) of a venture to an investor. Normal profit refers to a situation in which the economic profit is zero.
Wage	A wage is monetary compensation paid by an employer to an employee in exchange for work done. Payment may be calculated as a fixed amount for each task completed (a task wage or piece rate), or at an hourly or daily rate, or based on an easily measured quantity of work done. Payment by wage contrasts with salaried work, in which the employer pays an arranged amount at steady intervals (such as a week or month) regardless of hours worked, with commission which conditions pay on individual performance, and with compensation based on the performance of the company as a whole.
Efficiency	Efficiency in general, describes the extent to which time, effort or cost is well used for the intended task or purpose. It is often used with the specific purpose of relaying the capability of a specific application of effort to produce a specific outcome effectively with a minimum amount or quantity of waste, expense, or unnecessary effort. 'Efficiency' has widely varying meanings in different disciplines.
Globalization	Globaliization is the process of integration across world-space arising from the interchange of world views, products, ideas, and other aspects of culture. Advances in transportation and telecommunications infrastructure, including the rise of the telegraph and its posterity the Internet, are major factors in globalization, generating further interdependence of economic and cultural activities. Though scholars place the origins of globalization in modern times, others trace its history long before the European age of discovery and voyages to the New World.

1. What Is Economics?

CHAPTER HIGHLIGHTS & NOTES: KEY TERMS, PEOPLE, PLACES, CONCEPTS

Invisible hand	In economics, the invisible hand of the market is a metaphor conceived by Adam Smith to describe the self-regulating behavior of the marketplace. Individuals can make profit, and maximize it without the need for government intervention. The exact phrase is used just three times in Smith's writings, but has come to capture his important claim that individuals' efforts to maximize their own gains in a free market may benefit society, even if the ambitious have no benevolent intentions.
Bank	A bank is a financial institution and a financial intermediary that accepts deposits and channels those deposits into lending activities, either directly by loaning or indirectly through capital markets. A bank links together customers that have capital deficits and customers with capital surpluses. Due to their influential status within the financial system and upon national economies, banks are highly regulated in most countries.
Climate change	Climate change is a significant and lasting change in the statistical distribution of weather patterns over periods ranging from decades to millions of years. It may be a change in average weather conditions, or in the distribution of weather around the average conditions (i.e., more or fewer extreme weather events). Climate change is caused by factors such as biotic processes, variations in solar radiation received by Earth, plate tectonics, and volcanic eruptions.
Monopoly	A monopoly (from Greek monos μ???? + polein p??e?? (to sell)) exists when a specific person or enterprise is the only supplier of a particular commodity (this contrasts with a monopsony which relates to a single entity's control of a market to purchase a good or service, and with oligopoly which consists of a few entities dominating an industry). Monopolies are thus characterized by a lack of economic competition to produce the good or service and a lack of viable substitute goods. The verb 'monopolize' refers to the process by which a company gains the ability to raise prices or exclude competitors.
Mixed economies	A mixed economy is an economic system in which both the private sector and state direct the economy, reflecting characteristics of both market economies and planned economies. Most mixed economies can be described as market economies with strong regulatory oversight, and many mixed economies feature a variety of government-run enterprises and governmental provision of public goods. The basic idea of the mixed economy is that the means of production are mainly under private ownership; that markets remain the dominant form of economic coordination; and that profit-seeking enterprises and the accumulation of capital remains the fundamental driving force behind economic activity.
Opportunity cost	In microeconomic theory, the opportunity cost of a choice is the value of the best alternative forgone, in a situation in which a choice needs to be made between several mutually exclusive alternatives given limited resources. Assuming the best choice is made, it is the 'cost' incurred by not enjoying the benefit that would be had by taking the second best choice available.

1. What Is Economics?

CHAPTER HIGHLIGHTS & NOTES: KEY TERMS, PEOPLE, PLACES, CONCEPTS

Margin	In economics, a margin is a set of constraints conceptualised as a border. A marginal change is the change associated with a relaxation or tightening of constraints -- either change of the constraints, or a change in response to this change of the constraints.
Marginal cost	In economics and finance, marginal cost is the change in the total cost that arises when the quantity produced has an increment by unit. That is, it is the cost of producing one more unit of a good. In general terms, marginal cost at each level of production includes any additional costs required to produce the next unit.
Economic model	In economics, a model is a theoretical construct representing economic processes by a set of variables and a set of logical and/or quantitative relationships between them. The economic model is a simplified framework designed to illustrate complex processes, often but not always using mathematical techniques. Frequently, economic models posit structural parameters.
Normative statement	In economics, a normative statement expresses a value judgement about whether a situation is subjectively desirable or undesirable. 'The world would be a better place if the moon were made of green cheese' is a normative statement because it expresses a judgement about what ought to be. Notice that there is no way of testing the veracity of the statement; even if you disagree with it, you have no sure way of proving to someone who believes the statement that he or she is wrong by mere appeal to facts.
Positive statement	In economics and philosophy, a positive statement concerns what 'is', 'was', or 'will be', and contains no indication of approval or disapproval . Positive statements are testable - or, at least, it is possible to imagine facts that disprove them - but can be factually incorrect: 'The moon is made of black and gold cheese' is empirically false, but is still a positive statement, as it is a statement about what is, not what should be. Positive statements are contrasted with normative statements, which do make value judgements.
Causation	Causation is a belief that events occur in predictable ways and that one event leads to another. If the relationship between the variables is non-spurious (there is not a third variable causing the effect), the temporal order is in line (cause before effect), and the study is longitudinal, it may be deduced that it is a causal relationship.
Correlation	In statistics, dependence is any statistical relationship between two random variables or two sets of data. Correlation refers to any of a broad class of statistical relationships involving dependence. Familiar examples of dependent phenomena include the correlation between the physical statures of parents and their offspring, and the correlation between the demand for a product and its price.
Point	Points, sometimes also called 'discount points', are a form of pre-paid interest. One point equals one percent of the loan amount. By charging a borrower points, a lender effectively increases the yield on the loan above the amount of the stated interest rate.

1. What Is Economics?

CHAPTER HIGHLIGHTS & NOTES: KEY TERMS, PEOPLE, PLACES, CONCEPTS

Ceteris paribus	Ceteris paribus or caeteris paribus is a Latin phrase meaning 'with other things the same' or 'all other things being equal or held constant.' As an ablative absolute, it is commonly posed to mean 'all other things being equal.' A prediction or a statement about causal, empirical, or logical relation between two states of affairs is ceteris paribus via acknowledgement that the prediction can fail or the relation can be abolished by intervening factors.

A ceteris paribus assumption is often key to scientific inquiry, as scientists seek to screen out factors that perturb a relation of interest. Thus, epidemiologists seek to control independent variables as factors that may influence dependent variables--the outcomes or effects of interest. |
| Money | Monetary disequilibrium theory is basically a product of the Monetarist school mainly represented in the works of Leland Yeager and Austrian macroeconomics. The basic concept of monetary equilibrium (disequilibrium) was, however, defined in terms of an individual's demand for cash balance by Mises (1912) in his Theory of Money and Credit.

Monetary Disequilibrium is one of three theories of macroeconomic fluctuations which accord an important role to money, the others being the Austrian theory of the business cycle and one based on rational expectations. |

CHAPTER QUIZ: KEY TERMS, PEOPLE, PLACES, CONCEPTS

1. Not to be confused with Disgruntled worker.

   In economics, a _____ is a person of legal employment age who is not actively seeking employment or who does not find employment after long-term unemployment. This is usually because an individual has given up looking or has had no success in finding a job, hence the term 'discouraged'.

   a. Base period
   b. Benefit incidence
   c. Discouraged worker
   d. Bond

2. . A _____ is a financial institution and a financial intermediary that accepts deposits and channels those deposits into lending activities, either directly by loaning or indirectly through capital markets. A _____ links together customers that have capital deficits and customers with capital surpluses.

   Due to their influential status within the financial system and upon national economies, _____s are highly regulated in most countries.

1. What Is Economics?

CHAPTER QUIZ: KEY TERMS, PEOPLE, PLACES, CONCEPTS

   a. Bank
   b. Bank failure
   c. Jewish Social Democratic Party
   d. Bundism

3. A _____(ies) is an economic system in which both the private sector and state direct the economy, reflecting characteristics of both market economies and planned economies. Most _____ can be described as market economies with strong regulatory oversight, and many _____ feature a variety of government-run enterprises and governmental provision of public goods.

   The basic idea of the _____(ies) is that the means of production are mainly under private ownership; that markets remain the dominant form of economic coordination; and that profit-seeking enterprises and the accumulation of capital remains the fundamental driving force behind economic activity.

   a. Mixed economies
   b. Bankruptcy
   c. Benefit shortfall
   d. Climate change

4. In accountancy, _____ refers to two aspects of the same concept:•the decrease in value of assets (fair value _____), and•the allocation of the cost of assets to periods in which the assets are used (_____ with the matching principle).

   The former affects the balance sheet of a business or entity, and the latter affects the net income that they report. Generally the cost is allocated, as _____ expense, among the periods in which the asset is expected to be used. This expense is recognized by businesses for financial reporting and tax purposes.

   a. tax rate
   b. subsidy
   c. Depreciation
   d. Backup withholding

5. . In microeconomic theory, the _____ of a choice is the value of the best alternative forgone, in a situation in which a choice needs to be made between several mutually exclusive alternatives given limited resources. Assuming the best choice is made, it is the 'cost' incurred by not enjoying the benefit that would be had by taking the second best choice available. The New Oxford American Dictionary defines it as 'the loss of potential gain from other alternatives when one alternative is chosen'.

   a. In Time
   b. Endangered Species Act
   c. Energy Task Force

ANSWER KEY
1. What Is Economics?

1. c
2. a
3. a
4. c
5. d

You can take the complete Online Interactive Chapter Practice Test

for 1. What Is Economics?
on all key terms, persons, places, and concepts.

No Additional Costs

http://www.Cram101.com

Register, send an email request to Travis.Reese@Cram101.com to get your user Id and password.

Include your customer order number, and ISBN number from your studyguide Retailer.

2. The Economic Problem

CHAPTER OUTLINE: KEY TERMS, PEOPLE, PLACES, CONCEPTS

	Production possibilities frontier
	Scarcity
	Cost
	Opportunity cost
	Production
	Allocative efficiency
	Marginal cost
	Capital accumulation
	Economic growth
	Standard of living
	Technological change
	Absolute advantage
	Comparative advantage
	Specialization
	Factor market
	Market
	Money
	Circular flow
	Good

2. The Economic Problem

CHAPTER HIGHLIGHTS & NOTES: KEY TERMS, PEOPLE, PLACES, CONCEPTS

Production possibilities frontier	In economics, a production-possibility frontier, sometimes called a production-possibility curve, production-possibility boundary or product transformation curve, is a graph that shows the various combinations of amounts that two commodities could produce using the same fixed total amount of each of the factors of production. Graphically bounding the production set for fixed input quantities, the production possibilities frontier curve shows the maximum possible production level of one commodity for any given production level of the other, given the existing state of technology. By doing so, it defines productive efficiency in the context of that production set: a point on the frontier indicates efficient use of the available inputs, while a point beneath the curve indicates inefficiency.
Scarcity	Scarcity is the fundamental economic problem of having seemingly unlimited human wants in a world of limited resources. It states that society has insufficient productive resources to fulfill all human wants and needs. Additionally, scarcity implies that not all of society's goals can be pursued at the same time; trade-offs are made of one good against others.
Cost	In production, research, retail, and accounting, a cost is the value of money that has been used up to produce something, and hence is not available for use anymore. In business, the cost may be one of acquisition, in which case the amount of money expended to acquire it is counted as cost. In this case, money is the input that is gone in order to acquire the thing.
Opportunity cost	In microeconomic theory, the opportunity cost of a choice is the value of the best alternative forgone, in a situation in which a choice needs to be made between several mutually exclusive alternatives given limited resources. Assuming the best choice is made, it is the 'cost' incurred by not enjoying the benefit that would be had by taking the second best choice available. The New Oxford American Dictionary defines it as 'the loss of potential gain from other alternatives when one alternative is chosen'.
Production	Production is a process of combining various material inputs and immaterial inputs in order to make something for consumption (the output). It is the act of creating output, a good or service which has value and contributes to the utility of individuals. Economic well-being is created in a production process, meaning all economic activities that aim directly or indirectly to satisfy human needs.
Allocative efficiency	Allocative efficiency is a type of economic efficiency in which economy/producers produce only those types of goods and services that are more desirable in the society and also in high demand. According to the formula the point of allocative efficiency is a point where price is equal to marginal cost (P=MC)or (MC=MR). At this point the social surplus is maximized with no deadweight loss, or the value society puts on that level of output produced minus the value of resources used to achieve that level, yet can be applied to other things such as level of pollution.
Marginal cost	In economics and finance, marginal cost is the change in the total cost that arises when the quantity produced has an increment by unit. That is, it is the cost of producing one more unit of a good.

2. The Economic Problem

CHAPTER HIGHLIGHTS & NOTES: KEY TERMS, PEOPLE, PLACES, CONCEPTS

Capital accumulation	The accumulation of capital refers to the accumulation of capital, where capital is defined as money or a financial asset invested for the purpose of making more money . This activity forms the basis of the economic system of capitalism, where economic activity is structured around the accumulation of capital (investment in order to realize a financial profit). In a more broad sense, capital accumulation may refer to the gathering or amassing of any objects of value as judged by one's perceived reproductive interest group.
Economic growth	Economic growth is the increase in the market value of the goods and services produced by an economy over time. It is conventionally measured as the percent rate of increase in real gross domestic product, or real GDP. Of more importance is the growth of the ratio of GDP to population (GDP per capita), which is also called per capita income. An increase in per capita income is referred to as intensive growth.
Standard of living	Standard of living refers to the level of wealth, comfort, material goods and necessities available to a certain socioeconomic class in a certain geographic area. The standard of living includes factors such as income, quality and availability of employment, class disparity, poverty rate, quality and affordability of housing, hours of work required to purchase necessities, gross domestic product, inflation rate, number of holiday days per year, affordable (or free) access to quality healthcare, quality and availability of education, life expectancy, incidence of disease, cost of goods and services, infrastructure, national economic growth, economic and political and stability, political and religious freedom, environmental quality, climate and safety. The standard of living is closely related to quality of life.
Technological change	Technological change, technological development, technological achievement, or technological progress is the overall process of invention, innovation and diffusion of technology or processes. In essence technological change is the invention of technologies (including processes) and their commercialization via research and development (producing emerging technologies), the continual improvement of technologies (in which they often become less expensive), and the diffusion of technologies throughout industry or society (which sometimes involves disruption and convergence). In short, technological change is based on both better and more technology.
Absolute advantage	In economics, the principle of absolute advantage refers to the ability of a party to produce more of a good or service than competitors, using the same amount of resources. Adam Smith first described the principle of absolute advantage in the context of international trade, using labor as the only input. Since absolute advantage is determined by a simple comparison of labor productivities, it is possible for a party to have no absolute advantage in anything; in that case, according to the theory of absolute advantage, no trade will occur with the other party.

2. The Economic Problem

CHAPTER HIGHLIGHTS & NOTES: KEY TERMS, PEOPLE, PLACES, CONCEPTS

Comparative advantage	In economics, comparative advantage refers to the ability of a party to produce a particular good or service at a lower marginal and opportunity cost over another. Even if one country is more efficient in the production of all goods (absolute advantage in all goods) than the other, both countries will still gain by trading with each other, as long as they have different relative efficiencies. For example, if, using machinery, a worker in one country can produce both shoes and shirts at 6 per hour, and a worker in a country with less machinery can produce either 2 shoes or 4 shirts in an hour, each country can gain from trade because their internal trade-offs between shoes and shirts are different.
Specialization	Specialization is the separation of tasks within a system. In a multicellular creature, cells are specialized for functions such as bone construction or oxygen transport. In capitalist societies, individual workers specialize for functions such as building construction or gasoline transport.
Factor market	In economics a factor market refers to markets where services of the factors of production are bought and sold such as the labor markets, the capital market, the market for raw materials, and the market for management or entrepreneurial resources. Firms buy productive resources in return for making factor payments at factor prices. The interaction between product and factor markets involves the principle of derived demand.
Market	A financial market is a market in which people and entities can trade financial securities, commodities, and other fungible items of value at low transaction costs and at prices that reflect supply and demand. Securities include stocks and bonds, and commodities include precious metals or agricultural goods. There are both general markets (where many commodities are traded) and specialized markets (where only one commodity is traded).
Money	Monetary disequilibrium theory is basically a product of the Monetarist school mainly represented in the works of Leland Yeager and Austrian macroeconomics. The basic concept of monetary equilibrium (disequilibrium) was, however, defined in terms of an individual's demand for cash balance by Mises (1912) in his Theory of Money and Credit. Monetary Disequilibrium is one of three theories of macroeconomic fluctuations which accord an important role to money, the others being the Austrian theory of the business cycle and one based on rational expectations.
Circular flow	In economics, the terms circular flow of income or circular flow refer to a simple economic model which describes the reciprocal circulation of income between producers and consumers.

2. The Economic Problem

CHAPTER HIGHLIGHTS & NOTES: KEY TERMS, PEOPLE, PLACES, CONCEPTS

	In the circular flow model, the inter-dependent entities of producer and consumer are referred to as 'firms' and 'households' respectively and provide each other with factors in order to facilitate the flow of income. Firms provide consumers with goods and services in exchange for consumer expenditure and 'factors of production' from households.
Good	In economics, a good is a material that satisfies human wants and provides utility, for example, to a consumer making a purchase. A common distinction is made between 'goods' that are tangible property (also called goods) and services, which are non-physical. Commodities may be used as a synonym for economic goods but often refer to marketable raw materials and primary products.

CHAPTER QUIZ: KEY TERMS, PEOPLE, PLACES, CONCEPTS

1. _____ refers to the level of wealth, comfort, material goods and necessities available to a certain socioeconomic class in a certain geographic area. The _____ includes factors such as income, quality and availability of employment, class disparity, poverty rate, quality and affordability of housing, hours of work required to purchase necessities, gross domestic product, inflation rate, number of holiday days per year, affordable (or free) access to quality healthcare, quality and availability of education, life expectancy, incidence of disease, cost of goods and services, infrastructure, national economic growth, economic and political and stability, political and religious freedom, environmental quality, climate and safety. The _____ is closely related to quality of life.

    a. Bad bank
    b. Bank failure
    c. Standard of living
    d. Communist Bund

2. _____ is the increase in the market value of the goods and services produced by an economy over time. It is conventionally measured as the percent rate of increase in real gross domestic product, or real GDP. Of more importance is the growth of the ratio of GDP to population (GDP per capita), which is also called per capita income. An increase in per capita income is referred to as intensive growth.

    a. Bad bank
    b. Bank failure
    c. Economic growth
    d. Bundism

3. . In economics, a production-possibility frontier, sometimes called a production-possibility curve, production-possibility boundary or product transformation curve, is a graph that shows the various combinations of amounts that two commodities could produce using the same fixed total amount of each of the factors of production.

2. The Economic Problem

CHAPTER QUIZ: KEY TERMS, PEOPLE, PLACES, CONCEPTS

Graphically bounding the production set for fixed input quantities, the _____ curve shows the maximum possible production level of one commodity for any given production level of the other, given the existing state of technology. By doing so, it defines productive efficiency in the context of that production set: a point on the frontier indicates efficient use of the available inputs, while a point beneath the curve indicates inefficiency.

   a. quantity theory of money
   b. Production possibilities frontier
   c. money creation
   d. Dual-beta

4. In production, research, retail, and accounting, a _____ is the value of money that has been used up to produce something, and hence is not available for use anymore. In business, the _____ may be one of acquisition, in which case the amount of money expended to acquire it is counted as _____. In this case, money is the input that is gone in order to acquire the thing.

   a. cost reduction
   b. Cost
   c. Fuel protests in the United Kingdom
   d. 2010 student protest in Dublin

5. _____ is the separation of tasks within a system. In a multicellular creature, cells are specialized for functions such as bone construction or oxygen transport. In capitalist societies, individual workers specialize for functions such as building construction or gasoline transport.

   a. Capacity utilization
   b. Constant elasticity of substitution
   c. Specialization
   d. Cost-of-production theory of value

ANSWER KEY
2. The Economic Problem

1. c
2. c
3. b
4. b
5. c

You can take the complete Online Interactive Chapter Practice Test

for 2. The Economic Problem
on all key terms, persons, places, and concepts.

No Additional Costs

http://www.Cram101.com

Register, send an email request to Travis.Reese@Cram101.com to get your user Id and password.

Include your customer order number, and ISBN number from your studyguide Retailer.

3. Demand and Supply

CHAPTER OUTLINE: KEY TERMS, PEOPLE, PLACES, CONCEPTS

_____	Relative price
_____	Cost
_____	Factors of production
_____	Index
_____	Market
_____	Money
_____	Opportunity cost
_____	Price
_____	Production
_____	Demand
_____	Demand curve
_____	Law of demand
_____	Good
_____	Income
_____	Law of supply
_____	Marginal cost
_____	Supply
_____	Supply curve
_____	Technological change
_____	Quantitative easing
_____	Price level

3. Demand and Supply
CHAPTER OUTLINE: KEY TERMS, PEOPLE, PLACES, CONCEPTS

	Invisible hand
	Wealth
	Wealth of Nations

CHAPTER HIGHLIGHTS & NOTES: KEY TERMS, PEOPLE, PLACES, CONCEPTS

Relative price	A relative price is the price of a commodity such as a good or service in terms of another; i.e., the ratio of two prices. A relative price may be expressed in terms of a ratio between any two prices or the ratio between the price of one particular good and a weighted average of all other goods available in the market. A relative price is an opportunity cost.
Cost	In production, research, retail, and accounting, a cost is the value of money that has been used up to produce something, and hence is not available for use anymore. In business, the cost may be one of acquisition, in which case the amount of money expended to acquire it is counted as cost. In this case, money is the input that is gone in order to acquire the thing.
Factors of production	In economics, factors of production are the inputs to the production process. Finished goods are the output. Input determines the quantity of output i.e. output depends upon input.
Index	In economics and finance, an index is a statistical measure of changes in a representative group of individual data points. These data may be derived from any number of sources, including company performance, prices, productivity, and employment. Economic indices (index, plural) track economic health from different perspectives.
Market	A financial market is a market in which people and entities can trade financial securities, commodities, and other fungible items of value at low transaction costs and at prices that reflect supply and demand. Securities include stocks and bonds, and commodities include precious metals or agricultural goods. There are both general markets (where many commodities are traded) and specialized markets (where only one commodity is traded).
Money	Monetary disequilibrium theory is basically a product of the Monetarist school mainly represented in the works of Leland Yeager and Austrian macroeconomics.

3. Demand and Supply

CHAPTER HIGHLIGHTS & NOTES: KEY TERMS, PEOPLE, PLACES, CONCEPTS

	The basic concept of monetary equilibrium (disequilibrium) was, however, defined in terms of an individual's demand for cash balance by Mises (1912) in his Theory of Money and Credit.
	Monetary Disequilibrium is one of three theories of macroeconomic fluctuations which accord an important role to money, the others being the Austrian theory of the business cycle and one based on rational expectations.
Opportunity cost	In microeconomic theory, the opportunity cost of a choice is the value of the best alternative forgone, in a situation in which a choice needs to be made between several mutually exclusive alternatives given limited resources. Assuming the best choice is made, it is the 'cost' incurred by not enjoying the benefit that would be had by taking the second best choice available. The New Oxford American Dictionary defines it as 'the loss of potential gain from other alternatives when one alternative is chosen'.
Price	In ordinary usage, price is the quantity of payment or compensation given by one party to another in return for goods or services.
	In modern economies, prices are generally expressed in units of some form of currency. (For commodities, they are expressed as currency per unit weight of the commodity, e.g. euros per kilogram).
Production	Production is a process of combining various material inputs and immaterial inputs in order to make something for consumption (the output). It is the act of creating output, a good or service which has value and contributes to the utility of individuals. Economic well-being is created in a production process, meaning all economic activities that aim directly or indirectly to satisfy human needs.
Demand	In economics, demand for a good or service is an entire listing of the quantity of the good or service that a market would choose to buy, for every possible market price of the good or service. (Note: This distinguishes 'demand' from 'quantity demanded', where demand is a listing or graphing of quantity demanded at each possible price. In contrast to demand, quantity demanded is the exact quantity demanded at a certain price.
Demand curve	In economics, the demand curve is the graph depicting the relationship between the price of a certain commodity and the amount of it that consumers are willing and able to purchase at that given price. It is a graphic representation of a demand schedule. The demand curve for all consumers together follows from the demand curve of every individual consumer: the individual demands at each price are added together.
Law of demand	In economics, the law states that, all else being equal, as the price of a product increases, quantity demanded falls; likewise, as the price of a product decreases, quantity demanded increases.

3. Demand and Supply

CHAPTER HIGHLIGHTS & NOTES: KEY TERMS, PEOPLE, PLACES, CONCEPTS

	In other words, the law of demand states that the quantity demanded and the price of a commodity are inversely related, other things remaining constant. If the income of the consumer, prices of the related goods, and preferences of the consumer remain unchanged, then the change in quantity of good demanded by the consumer will be negatively correlated to the change in the price of the good.
Good	In economics, a good is a material that satisfies human wants and provides utility, for example, to a consumer making a purchase. A common distinction is made between 'goods' that are tangible property (also called goods) and services, which are non-physical. Commodities may be used as a synonym for economic goods but often refer to marketable raw materials and primary products.
Income	Income is the consumption and savings opportunity gained by an entity within a specified timeframe, which is generally expressed in monetary terms. However, for households and individuals, 'income is the sum of all the wages, salaries, profits, interests payments, rents and other forms of earnings received... in a given period of time.' In the field of public economics, the term may refer to the accumulation of both monetary and non-monetary consumption ability, with the former (monetary) being used as a proxy for total income.
Law of supply	The law of supply is a fundamental principle of economic theory which states that, all else equal, an increase in price results in an increase in quantity supplied. In other words, there is a direct relationship between price and quantity: quantities respond in the same direction as price changes. This means that producers are willing to offer more products for sale on the market at higher prices by increasing production as a way of increasing profits.
Marginal cost	In economics and finance, marginal cost is the change in the total cost that arises when the quantity produced has an increment by unit. That is, it is the cost of producing one more unit of a good. In general terms, marginal cost at each level of production includes any additional costs required to produce the next unit.
Supply	In economics, supply refers to the amount of a product that producers and firms are willing to sell at a given price all other factors being held constant. Usually, supply is plotted as a supply curve showing the relationship of price to the amount of product businesses are willing to sell
Supply curve	In microeconomics, supply and demand is an economic model of price determination in a market. It concludes that in a competitive market, the unit price for a particular good will vary until it settles at a point where the quantity demanded by consumers (at current price) will equal the quantity supplied by producers (at current price), resulting in an economic equilibrium for price and quantity.

3. Demand and Supply

CHAPTER HIGHLIGHTS & NOTES: KEY TERMS, PEOPLE, PLACES, CONCEPTS

Technological change	Technological change, technological development, technological achievement, or technological progress is the overall process of invention, innovation and diffusion of technology or processes. In essence technological change is the invention of technologies (including processes) and their commercialization via research and development (producing emerging technologies), the continual improvement of technologies (in which they often become less expensive), and the diffusion of technologies throughout industry or society (which sometimes involves disruption and convergence). In short, technological change is based on both better and more technology.
Quantitative easing	Quantitative easing is an unconventional monetary policy used by central banks to stimulate the economy when standard monetary policy has become ineffective. A central bank implements quantitative easing by buying specified amounts of financial assets from commercial banks and other private institutions, thus raising the prices of those financial assets and lowering their yield, while simultaneously increasing the monetary base. This is distinguished from the more usual policy of buying or selling short term government bonds in order to keep interbank interest rates at a specified target value.
Price level	The general price level is a hypothetical measure of overall prices for some set of goods and services, in a given region during a given interval, normalized relative to some base set. Typically, a price level is approximated with a price index.
Invisible hand	In economics, the invisible hand of the market is a metaphor conceived by Adam Smith to describe the self-regulating behavior of the marketplace. Individuals can make profit, and maximize it without the need for government intervention. The exact phrase is used just three times in Smith's writings, but has come to capture his important claim that individuals' efforts to maximize their own gains in a free market may benefit society, even if the ambitious have no benevolent intentions.
Wealth	The modern understanding of Wealth is the abundance of valuable resources or material possessions. This excludes the core meaning as held in the originating old English word weal, which is from an Indo-European word stem. In this larger understanding of wealth, an individual, community, region or country that possesses an abundance of such possessions or resources to the benefit of the common good is known as wealthy.
Wealth of Nations	An Inquiry into the Nature and Causes of the Wealth of Nations, generally referred to by its shortened title The Wealth of Nations, is the magnum opus of the Scottish economist and moral philosopher Adam Smith. First published in 1776, the book offers one of the world's first collected descriptions of what builds nations' wealth and is today a fundamental work in classical economics. Through reflection over the economics at the beginning of the Industrial Revolution the book touches upon such broad topics as the division of labour, productivity and free markets.

3. Demand and Supply

CHAPTER QUIZ: KEY TERMS, PEOPLE, PLACES, CONCEPTS

1. A financial _____ is a _____ in which people and entities can trade financial securities, commodities, and other fungible items of value at low transaction costs and at prices that reflect supply and demand. Securities include stocks and bonds, and commodities include precious metals or agricultural goods.

    There are both general _____s (where many commodities are traded) and specialized _____s (where only one commodity is traded).

    a. Financial market
    b. Bad bank
    c. Bank failure
    d. Market

2. In ordinary usage, _____ is the quantity of payment or compensation given by one party to another in return for goods or services.

    In modern economies, _____s are generally expressed in units of some form of currency. (For commodities, they are expressed as currency per unit weight of the commodity, e.g. euros per kilogram).

    a. Balloon payment mortgage
    b. Bid price
    c. Price
    d. Capitalization rate

3. In economics, _____ refers to the amount of a product that producers and firms are willing to sell at a given price all other factors being held constant. Usually, _____ is plotted as a _____ curve showing the relationship of price to the amount of product businesses are willing to sell.

    a. Base period
    b. Benefit incidence
    c. Blanket order
    d. Supply

4. In economics and finance, an _____ is a statistical measure of changes in a representative group of individual data points. These data may be derived from any number of sources, including company performance, prices, productivity, and employment. Economic indices (_____, plural) track economic health from different perspectives.

    a. Boomtown
    b. Clean growth
    c. Community capitalism
    d. Index

5. . Monetary disequilibrium theory is basically a product of the Monetarist school mainly represented in the works of Leland Yeager and Austrian macroeconomics.

3. Demand and Supply

CHAPTER QUIZ: KEY TERMS, PEOPLE, PLACES, CONCEPTS

The basic concept of monetary equilibrium (disequilibrium) was, however, defined in terms of an individual's demand for cash balance by Mises (1912) in his Theory of _____ and Credit.

Monetary Disequilibrium is one of three theories of macroeconomic fluctuations which accord an important role to _____, the others being the Austrian theory of the business cycle and one based on rational expectations.

a. Break-even
b. Broad money
c. Money
d. Cash-in-advance constraint

ANSWER KEY
3. Demand and Supply

1. d
2. c
3. d
4. d
5. c

You can take the complete Online Interactive Chapter Practice Test

for 3. Demand and Supply
on all key terms, persons, places, and concepts.

No Additional Costs

http://www.Cram101.com

Register, send an email request to Travis.Reese@Cram101.com to get your user Id and password.

Include your customer order number, and ISBN number from your studyguide Retailer.

4. Measuring GDP and Economic Growth

CHAPTER OUTLINE: KEY TERMS, PEOPLE, PLACES, CONCEPTS

- Double counting
- Good
- Gros
- Gross domestic product
- Intermediate good
- Market value
- Circular flow
- Income
- Product
- Service
- Aggregate income
- Household
- Investment
- Consumption
- Aggregate expenditure
- Depreciation
- Export
- Gross profit
- Net investment
- Bureau of Economic Analysis
- Gross private domestic investment

4. Measuring GDP and Economic Growth
CHAPTER OUTLINE: KEY TERMS, PEOPLE, PLACES, CONCEPTS

- National income
- National Income and Product Accounts
- Personal consumption
- Transfer payment
- Deflator
- Indirect tax
- Subsidies
- Income approach
- Index
- Market
- Price
- Real GDP
- Standard of living
- Use
- Business cycle
- Recession
- Purchasing power
- Purchasing power parity
- Management
- Underground economy
- Economy

4. Measuring GDP and Economic Growth

CHAPTER OUTLINE: KEY TERMS, PEOPLE, PLACES, CONCEPTS

	Well-being
	Excess reserves

CHAPTER HIGHLIGHTS & NOTES: KEY TERMS, PEOPLE, PLACES, CONCEPTS

Double counting	Double counting in accounting is an error whereby a transaction is counted more than once, for whatever reason. But in social accounting it also refers to a conceptual problem in social accounting practice, when the attempt is made to estimate the new value added by Gross Output, or the value of total investments.
Good	In economics, a good is a material that satisfies human wants and provides utility, for example, to a consumer making a purchase. A common distinction is made between 'goods' that are tangible property (also called goods) and services, which are non-physical. Commodities may be used as a synonym for economic goods but often refer to marketable raw materials and primary products.
Gros	A gros was a type of silver coinage of France from the time of Saint Louis. There were gros tournois and gros parisis. The gros was sub-divided in half gros and quarter gros.
Gross domestic product	Gross domestic product is the market value of all officially recognized final goods and services produced within a country in a year, or other given period of time. gross domestic product per capita is often considered an indicator of a country's standard of living. gross domestic product per capita is not a measure of personal income .
Intermediate good	Intermediate goods or producer goods or semi-finished products are goods used as inputs in the production of other goods, such as partly finished goods. Also, they are goods used in production of final goods. A firm may make and then use intermediate goods, or make and then sell, or buy then use them.
Market value	Market value or OMV is the price at which an asset would trade in a competitive auction setting. Market value is often used interchangeably with open market value, fair value or fair market value, although these terms have distinct definitions in different standards, and may differ in some circumstances.
Circular flow	In economics, the terms circular flow of income or circular flow refer to a simple economic model which describes the reciprocal circulation of income between producers and consumers.

4. Measuring GDP and Economic Growth

CHAPTER HIGHLIGHTS & NOTES: KEY TERMS, PEOPLE, PLACES, CONCEPTS

	In the circular flow model, the inter-dependent entities of producer and consumer are referred to as 'firms' and 'households' respectively and provide each other with factors in order to facilitate the flow of income. Firms provide consumers with goods and services in exchange for consumer expenditure and 'factors of production' from households.
Income	Income is the consumption and savings opportunity gained by an entity within a specified timeframe, which is generally expressed in monetary terms. However, for households and individuals, 'income is the sum of all the wages, salaries, profits, interests payments, rents and other forms of earnings received... in a given period of time.'
	In the field of public economics, the term may refer to the accumulation of both monetary and non-monetary consumption ability, with the former (monetary) being used as a proxy for total income.
Product	In marketing, a product is anything that can be offered to a market that might satisfy a want or need. In retailing, products are called merchandise. In manufacturing, products are bought as raw materials and sold as finished goods.
Service	In economics, a service is an intangible commodity. That is, services are an example of intangible economic goods.
	Service provision is often an economic activity where the buyer does not generally, except by exclusive contract, obtain exclusive ownership of the thing purchased.
Aggregate income	Aggregate income is the combined income earned by an entire group of persons. 'Aggregate income' in economics is a broad conceptual term. It may express the proceeds from total output in the economy for producers of that output.
Household	A household consists of one or more people who live in the same dwelling and also share at meals or living accommodation, and may consist of a single family or some other grouping of people. A single dwelling will be considered to contain multiple households if meals or living space are not shared. The household is the basic unit of analysis in many social, microeconomic and government models, and is important to the fields of economics, inheritance.
Investment	Investment is time, energy, or matter spent in the hope of future benefits. Investment has different meanings in economics and finance.
	In economics, investment is the accumulation of newly produced physical entities, such as factories, machinery, houses, and goods inventories.
Consumption	Consumption is a major concept in economics and is also studied by many other social sciences. Economists are particularly interested in the relationship between consumption and income, and therefore in economics the consumption function plays a major role.

4. Measuring GDP and Economic Growth

CHAPTER HIGHLIGHTS & NOTES: KEY TERMS, PEOPLE, PLACES, CONCEPTS

Aggregate expenditure	In economics, Aggregate Expenditure is a measure of national income. Aggregate Expenditure is defined as the current value of all the finished goods and services in the economy. The aggregate expenditure is thus the sum total of all the expenditures undertaken in the economy by the factors during a given time period.
Depreciation	In accountancy, depreciation refers to two aspects of the same concept:•the decrease in value of assets (fair value depreciation), and•the allocation of the cost of assets to periods in which the assets are used (depreciation with the matching principle). The former affects the balance sheet of a business or entity, and the latter affects the net income that they report. Generally the cost is allocated, as depreciation expense, among the periods in which the asset is expected to be used. This expense is recognized by businesses for financial reporting and tax purposes.
Export	The term export means shipping the goods and services out of the port of a country. The seller of such goods and services is referred to as an 'exporter' who is based in the country of export whereas the overseas based buyer is referred to as an 'importer'. In International Trade, 'exports' refers to selling goods and services produced in the home country to other markets.
Gross profit	In accounting, gross profit or sales profit is the difference between revenue and the cost of making a product or providing a service, before deducting overhead, payroll, taxation, and interest payments. Note that this is different from operating profit (earnings before interest and taxes). The various deductions (and their corresponding metrics) leading from Net sales to Net income are as follow:Net sales = Gross sales - (Customer Discounts, Returns, Allowances)Gross profit = Net sales - Cost of goods soldGross profit percentage = {(Net sales - Cost of goods sold)/Net sales} x 100Operating Profit = Gross Profit - Total operating expensesNet income (or Net profit) = Operating Profit - taxes - interest (Note: cost of goods sold is calculated differently for a merchandising business than for a manufacturer).
Net investment	In economics, net investment refers to an activity of spending which increases the availability of fixed capital goods or means of production. It is the total spending on new fixed investment minus replacement investment, which simply replaces depreciated capital goods. Net Investment is equal to the Gross investment minus depreciation
Bureau of Economic Analysis	The Bureau of Economic Analysis is an agency in the United States Department of Commerce that provides important economic statistics including the gross domestic product of the United States. BEA is a principal agency of the U.S. Federal Statistical System. Its stated mission is to 'promote a better understanding of the U.S.

4. Measuring GDP and Economic Growth

CHAPTER HIGHLIGHTS & NOTES: KEY TERMS, PEOPLE, PLACES, CONCEPTS

Gross private domestic investment	Gross private domestic investment is the measure of investment used to compute GDP in economic measurement of nations. This is an important component of GDP because it provides an indicator of the future productive capacity of the economy. It includes replacement purchases plus net additions to capital assets plus investments in inventories.
National income	A variety of measures of national income and output are used in economics to estimate total economic activity in a country or region, including gross domestic product, gross national product (GNP), net national income and adjusted national income. All are specially concerned with counting the total amount of goods and services produced within some 'boundary'. The boundary is usually defined by geography or citizenship, and may also restrict the goods and services that are counted.
National Income and Product Accounts	The national income and product accounts are part of the national accounts of the United States. They are produced by the Bureau of Economic Analysis of the Department of Commerce. They are one of the main sources of data on general economic activity in the United States.
Personal consumption	The Personal Consumption Expenditure measure is the component statistic for consumption in GDP collected by the BEA. It consists of the actual and imputed expenditures of households and includes data pertaining to durable and non-durable goods and services. It is essentially a measure of goods and services targeted towards individuals and consumed by individuals. The PCE price index (PCEPI), also referred to as the PCE deflator, PCE price deflator, or the Implicit Price Deflator for Personal Consumption Expenditures (IPD for PCE) by the BEA, and as the Chain-type Price Index for Personal Consumption Expenditures (CTPIPCE) by the FOMC, is a United States-wide indicator of the average increase in prices for all domestic personal consumption.
Transfer payment	In economics, a transfer payment is a redistribution of income in the market system. These payments are considered to be non-exhaustive because they do not directly absorb resources or create output. In other words, the transfer is made without any exchange of goods or services.
Deflator	In statistics, a deflator is a value that allows data to be measured over time in terms of some base period, usually through a price index, in order to distinguish between a changes in the money value of a gross national product that come from a change in prices, and changes from a change in physical output. It is the measure of the price level for some quantity. A deflator serves as a price index in which the effects of inflation are nulled.
Indirect tax	An indirect tax (such as sales tax, a specific tax, value added tax, or goods and services tax (GST)) is a tax collected by an intermediary (such as a retail store) from the person who bears the ultimate economic burden of the tax (such as the consumer). The intermediary later files a tax return and forwards the tax proceeds to government with the return.

4. Measuring GDP and Economic Growth

CHAPTER HIGHLIGHTS & NOTES: KEY TERMS, PEOPLE, PLACES, CONCEPTS

Subsidies	A subsidy is a form of financial or in kind support extended to an economic sector generally with the aim of promoting economic and social policy. Although commonly extended from Government, the term subsidy can relate to any type of support - for example from NGOs or implicit subsidies. Subsidies come in various forms including: direct (cash grants, interest-free loans) and indirect (tax breaks, insurance, low-interest loans, depreciation write-offs, rent rebates).
Income approach	The Income Approach is one of three major groups of methodologies, called valuation approaches, used by appraisers. It is particularly common in commercial real estate appraisal and in business appraisal. The fundamental math is similar to the methods used for financial valuation, securities analysis, or bond pricing.
Index	In economics and finance, an index is a statistical measure of changes in a representative group of individual data points. These data may be derived from any number of sources, including company performance, prices, productivity, and employment. Economic indices (index, plural) track economic health from different perspectives.
Market	A financial market is a market in which people and entities can trade financial securities, commodities, and other fungible items of value at low transaction costs and at prices that reflect supply and demand. Securities include stocks and bonds, and commodities include precious metals or agricultural goods. There are both general markets (where many commodities are traded) and specialized markets (where only one commodity is traded).
Price	In ordinary usage, price is the quantity of payment or compensation given by one party to another in return for goods or services. In modern economies, prices are generally expressed in units of some form of currency. (For commodities, they are expressed as currency per unit weight of the commodity, e.g. euros per kilogram).
Real GDP	Real Gross Domestic Product (real GDP) is a macroeconomic measure of the value of economic output adjusted for price changes . This adjustment transforms the money-value measure, nominal GDP, into an index for quantity of total output. GDP is the sum of consumer Spending, Investment made by industry, Excess of Exports over Imports and Government Spending.
Standard of living	Standard of living refers to the level of wealth, comfort, material goods and necessities available to a certain socioeconomic class in a certain geographic area.

4. Measuring GDP and Economic Growth

CHAPTER HIGHLIGHTS & NOTES: KEY TERMS, PEOPLE, PLACES, CONCEPTS

	The standard of living includes factors such as income, quality and availability of employment, class disparity, poverty rate, quality and affordability of housing, hours of work required to purchase necessities, gross domestic product, inflation rate, number of holiday days per year, affordable (or free) access to quality healthcare, quality and availability of education, life expectancy, incidence of disease, cost of goods and services, infrastructure, national economic growth, economic and political and stability, political and religious freedom, environmental quality, climate and safety. The standard of living is closely related to quality of life.
Use	Use, as a term in real property law of common law countries, amounts to a recognition of the duty of a person, to whom property has been conveyed for certain purposes, to carry out those purposes. Uses were equitable or beneficial interests in land. In early law a man could not dispose of his estate by will nor could religious houses acquire it.
Business cycle	The term business cycle refers to economy-wide fluctuations in production, trade and economic activity in general over several months or years in an economy organized on free-enterprise principles. The business cycle is the upward and downward movements of levels of GDP (gross domestic product) and refers to the period of expansions and contractions in the level of economic activities (business fluctuations) around its long-term growth trend. These fluctuations occur around a long-term growth trend, and typically involve shifts over time between periods of relatively rapid economic growth (an expansion or boom), and periods of relative stagnation or decline (a contraction or recession).
Recession	In economics, a recession is a business cycle contraction. It is a general slowdown in economic activity. Macroeconomic indicators such as GDP (gross domestic product), investment spending, capacity utilization, household income, business profits, and inflation fall, while bankruptcies and the unemployment rate rise.
Purchasing power	Purchasing power is the number of goods or services that can be purchased with a unit of currency. For example, if one had taken one unit of currency to a store in the 1950s, it is probablo that it would have been possible to buy a greater number of items than would today, indicating that one would have had a greater purchasing power in the 1950s. Currency can be either a commodity money, like gold or silver, or fiat currency, or free-floating market-valued currency like US dollars.
Purchasing power parity	Purchasing power parity is a component of some economic theories and is a technique used to determine the relative value of different currencies.

4. Measuring GDP and Economic Growth

CHAPTER HIGHLIGHTS & NOTES: KEY TERMS, PEOPLE, PLACES, CONCEPTS

	Theories that invoke purchasing power parity assume that in some circumstances (for example, as a long-run tendency) it would cost exactly the same number of, say, US dollars to buy euros and then to use the proceeds to buy a market basket of goods as it would cost to use those dollars directly in purchasing the market basket of goods.
	The concept of purchasing power parity allows one to estimate what the exchange rate between two currencies would have to be in order for the exchange to be at par with the purchasing power of the two countries' currencies.
Management	Management in businesses and other organizations, including not-for-profit organizations and government bodies, refers to the individuals who set the strategy of the organization and coordinate the efforts of employees to accomplish objectives by using available human, financial and other resources efficiently and effectively. Resourcing encompasses the deployment and manipulation of human resources, financial resources, technological resources, natural resources and other resources.
	Management is also an academic discipline, a social science whose objective is to study social organization and organizational leadership.
Underground economy	A black market or underground economy is the market in which goods or services are traded illegally. The key distinction of a black market trade is that the transaction itself is illegal. The goods or services may or may not themselves be illegal to own, or to trade through other, legal channels.
Economy	An economy or economic system consists of the production, distribution or trade, and consumption of limited goods and services by different agents in a given geographical location. The economic agents can be individuals, businesses, organizations, or governments. Transactions occur when two parties agree to the value or price of the transacted good or service, commonly expressed in a certain currency.
Well-being	Well-being or welfare is a general term for the condition of an individual or group, for example their social, economic, psychological, spiritual or medical state; high well-being means that, in some sense, the individual or group's experience is positive, while low well-being is associated with negative happenings.
	In economics, the term is used for one or more Quantitative measures intended to assess the quality of life of a group, for example, in the capabilities approach and the economics of happiness. Like the related cognate terms 'wealth' and 'welfare', economics sources may contrast the state with its opposite.
Excess reserves	In banking, excess reserves are bank reserves in excess of a reserve requirement set by a central bank. They are reserves of cash more than the required amounts.

4. Measuring GDP and Economic Growth

CHAPTER QUIZ: KEY TERMS, PEOPLE, PLACES, CONCEPTS

1. _____ is a major concept in economics and is also studied by many other social sciences. Economists are particularly interested in the relationship between _____ and income, and therefore in economics the _____ function plays a major role.

   Different schools of economists define production and _____ differently.

   a. Boukaseff scale
   b. Bureau de change
   c. Business cycle accounting
   d. Consumption

2. _____ is the combined income earned by an entire group of persons. '_____' in economics is a broad conceptual term. It may express the proceeds from total output in the economy for producers of that output.

   a. Aggregate income
   b. revenue
   c. Federal Reserve
   d. Fuel protests in the United Kingdom

3. The _____ are part of the national accounts of the United States. They are produced by the Bureau of Economic Analysis of the Department of Commerce. They are one of the main sources of data on general economic activity in the United States.

   a. Baker cube
   b. National Income and Product Accounts
   c. Benefitive treasury measure
   d. Bereavement benefit

4. _____ is the measure of investment used to compute GDP in economic measurement of nations. This is an important component of GDP because it provides an indicator of the future productive capacity of the economy. It includes replacement purchases plus net additions to capital assets plus investments in inventories.

   a. Capital account
   b. Capital formation
   c. Gross private domestic investment
   d. Domar aggregation

5. . _____ is the market value of all officially recognized final goods and services produced within a country in a year, or other given period of time. _____ per capita is often considered an indicator of a country's standard of living.

   _____ per capita is not a measure of personal income.

   a. Gross domestic product
   b. wage

4. Measuring GDP and Economic Growth

CHAPTER QUIZ: KEY TERMS, PEOPLE, PLACES, CONCEPTS

c. national income
d. Capital account

ANSWER KEY
4. Measuring GDP and Economic Growth

1. d
2. a
3. b
4. c
5. a

You can take the complete Online Interactive Chapter Practice Test

for 4. Measuring GDP and Economic Growth
on all key terms, persons, places, and concepts.

No Additional Costs

http://www.Cram101.com

Register, send an email request to Travis.Reese@Cram101.com to get your user Id and password.

Include your customer order number, and ISBN number from your studyguide Retailer.

5. Monitoring Jobs and Inflation

CHAPTER OUTLINE: KEY TERMS, PEOPLE, PLACES, CONCEPTS

	Bernanke
	Great Depression
	Human capital
	Money
	New Deal
	Tariff
	Trade
	Unemployment
	Labor force
	Rate
	Employment-to-population ratio
	Labor force participation rate
	Frictional unemployment
	Full employment
	Structural change
	Structural unemployment
	Distribution
	Efficiency wage
	Minimum wage
	Output gap
	Real GDP

5. Monitoring Jobs and Inflation
CHAPTER OUTLINE: KEY TERMS, PEOPLE, PLACES, CONCEPTS

	Unemployment benefits
	Wage
	Consumer price index
	Deflation
	Hyperinflation
	Inflation
	Price level
	Production
	Consumer
	Price index
	Price
	Purchasing power
	GDP deflator
	Personal consumption
	Deflator
	Core inflation
	Inflationary gap
	Macroeconomics
	Reserve
	Variable

5. Monitoring Jobs and Inflation

CHAPTER HIGHLIGHTS & NOTES: KEY TERMS, PEOPLE, PLACES, CONCEPTS

Bernanke	Ben Shalom Bernanke is an American economist at the Brookings Institution who served two terms as chairman of the Federal Reserve, the central bank of the United States from 2006 to 2014. During his tenure as chairman, Bernanke oversaw the Federal Reserve's response to the late-2000s financial crisis. Before becoming Federal Reserve chairman, Bernanke was a tenured professor at Princeton University and chaired the department of economics there from 1996 to September 2002, when he went on public service leave. From 2002 until 2005, he was a member of the Board of Governors of the Federal Reserve System, proposed the Bernanke Doctrine, and first discussed 'the Great Moderation' -- the theory that traditional business cycles have declined in volatility in recent decades through structural changes that have occurred in the international economy, particularly increases in the economic stability of developing nations, diminishing the influence of macroeconomic (monetary and fiscal) policy.
Great Depression	The Great Depression was a severe worldwide economic depression in the decade preceding World War II. The timing of the Great Depression varied across nations, but in most countries it started in 1930 and lasted until the late 1930s or middle 1940s. It was the longest, deepest, and most widespread depression of the 20th century. In the 21st century, the Great Depression is commonly used as an example of how far the world's economy can decline.
Human capital	Human capital is the stock of competencies, knowledge, habits, social and personality attributes, including creativity, cognitive abilities, embodied in the ability to perform labor so as to produce economic value. It is an aggregate economic view of the human being acting within economies, which is an attempt to capture the social, biological, cultural and psychological complexity as they interact in explicit and/or economic transactions. Many theories explicitly connect investment in human capital development to education, and the role of human capital in economic development, productivity growth, and innovation has frequently been cited as a justification for government subsidies for education and job skills training.
Money	Monetary disequilibrium theory is basically a product of the Monetarist school mainly represented in the works of Leland Yeager and Austrian macroeconomics. The basic concept of monetary equilibrium (disequilibrium) was, however, defined in terms of an individual's demand for cash balance by Mises (1912) in his Theory of Money and Credit. Monetary Disequilibrium is one of three theories of macroeconomic fluctuations which accord an important role to money, the others being the Austrian theory of the business cycle and one based on rational expectations.
New Deal	The New Deal was a series of domestic programs enacted in the United States between 1933 and 1936, and a few that came later.

5. Monitoring Jobs and Inflation

CHAPTER HIGHLIGHTS & NOTES: KEY TERMS, PEOPLE, PLACES, CONCEPTS

	They included both laws passed by Congress as well as presidential executive orders during the first term (1933-37) of President Franklin D. Roosevelt. The programs were in response to the Great Depression, and focused on what historians call the '3 Rs': Relief, Recovery, and Reform.
Tariff	A tariff is a tax on imports or exports (an international trade tariff), or a list of prices for such things as rail service, bus routes, and electrical usage (electrical tariff, etc).. The meaning in (1) is now the more common meaning. The meaning in (2) is historically earlier.
Trade	In finance, a trade is an exchange of a security for 'cash', typically a short-dated promise to pay in the currency of the country where the 'exchange' is located.
Unemployment	Unemployment occurs when people are without work and actively seeking work. The unemployment rate is a measure of the prevalence of unemployment and it is calculated as a percentage by dividing the number of unemployed individuals by all individuals currently in the labor force. During periods of recession, an economy usually experiences a relatively high unemployment rate.
Labor force	The labor force is the actual number of people available for work. The labor force of a country includes both the employed and the unemployed. The labor force participation rate, LFPR (or economic activity rate, EAR), is the ratio between the labor force and the overall size of their cohort (national population of the same age range).
Rate	In mathematics, a rate is a ratio between two measurements with different units. If the unit or quantity in respect of which something is changing is not specified, usually the rate is per unit time. However, a rate of change can be specified per unit time, or per unit of length or mass or another quantity.
Employment-to-population ratio	The Organization for Economic Co-operation and Development defines the employment rate as the employment-to-population ratio. The employment-population ratio is many American economists' favorite gauge of the American jobs picture. According to Paul Ashworth, chief North American economist for Capital Economics, 'The employment population ratio is the best measure of labor market conditions.' This is a statistical ratio that measures the proportion of the country's working-age population (ages 15 to 64 in most OECD countries) that is employed.
Labor force participation rate	The labor force is the actual number of people available for work. The labor force of a country includes both the employed and the unemployed. The labor force participation rate, labor force participation rate (or economic activity rate, EAR), is the ratio between the labor force and the overall size of their cohort (national population of the same age range).
Frictional unemployment	Frictional unemployment is the time period between jobs when a worker is searching for, or transitioning from one job to another. It is sometimes called search unemployment and can be voluntary based on the circumstances of the unemployed individual.

5. Monitoring Jobs and Inflation

CHAPTER HIGHLIGHTS & NOTES: KEY TERMS, PEOPLE, PLACES, CONCEPTS

Full employment	Full employment, in macroeconomics, is the level of employment rates where there is no cyclical or deficient-demand unemployment. It is defined by the majority of mainstream economists as being an acceptable level of unemployment somewhere above 0%. The discrepancy from 0% arises due to non-cyclical types of unemployment.
Structural change	Economic structural change refers to a long-term shift in the fundamental structure of an economy, which is often linked to growth and economic development. For example, a subsistence economy may be transformed into a manufacturing economy, or a regulated mixed economy is liberalized. A current driver of structural change in the world economy is globalization.
Structural unemployment	Structural unemployment is a form of unemployment where, at a given wage, the quantity of labor supplied exceeds the quantity of labor demanded, because there is a fundamental mismatch between the number of people who want to work and the number of jobs that are available. The unemployed workers may lack the skills needed for the jobs, or they may not live in the part of the country or world where the jobs are available. Structural unemployment is one of the five major categories of unemployment distinguished by economists.
Distribution	Distribution in economics refers to the way total output, income, or wealth is distributed among individuals or among the factors of production. In general theory and the national income and product accounts, each unit of output corresponds to a unit of income. One use of national accounts is for classifying factor incomes and measuring their respective shares, as in National Income.
Efficiency wage	In labor economics, the efficiency wage hypothesis argues that wages, at least in some markets, form in a way that is not market-clearing. Specifically, it points to the incentive for managers to pay their employees more than the market-clearing wage in order to increase their productivity or efficiency, or reduce costs associated with turnover, in industries where the costs of replacing labor is high. This increased labor productivity and/or decreased costs pay for the higher wages.
Minimum wage	A minimum wage is the lowest hourly, daily or monthly remuneration that employers may legally pay to workers. Equivalently, it is the lowest wage at which workers may sell their labor. Although minimum wage laws are in effect in many jurisdictions, differences of opinion exist about the benefits and drawbacks of a minimum wage.
Output gap	The GDP gap or the output gap is the difference between actual GDP or actual output and potential GDP. The calculation for the output gap is $Y-Y^*$ where Y is actual output and Y^* is potential output. If this calculation yields a positive number it is called an inflationary gap and indicates the growth of aggregate demand is outpacing the growth of aggregate supply--possibly creating inflation; if the calculation yields a negative number it is called a recessionary gap--possibly signifying deflation. The percentage GDP gap is the actual GDP minus the potential GDP divided by the potential GDP.

5. Monitoring Jobs and Inflation

CHAPTER HIGHLIGHTS & NOTES: KEY TERMS, PEOPLE, PLACES, CONCEPTS

$$\frac{(GDP_{actual} - GDP_{potential})}{GDP_{potential}}$$

Real GDP	Real Gross Domestic Product (real GDP) is a macroeconomic measure of the value of economic output adjusted for price changes. This adjustment transforms the money-value measure, nominal GDP, into an index for quantity of total output. GDP is the sum of consumer Spending, Investment made by industry, Excess of Exports over Imports and Government Spending.
Unemployment benefits	Unemployment benefits are social welfare payments made by the state or other authorised bodies to unemployed people. Benefits may be based on a compulsory para-governmental insurance system. Depending on the jurisdiction and the status of the person, those sums may be small, covering only basic needs, or may compensate the lost time proportionally to the previous earned salary.
Wage	A wage is monetary compensation paid by an employer to an employee in exchange for work done. Payment may be calculated as a fixed amount for each task completed (a task wage or piece rate), or at an hourly or daily rate, or based on an easily measured quantity of work done. Payment by wage contrasts with salaried work, in which the employer pays an arranged amount at steady intervals (such as a week or month) regardless of hours worked, with commission which conditions pay on individual performance, and with compensation based on the performance of the company as a whole.
Consumer price index	A consumer price index measures changes in the price level of a market basket of consumer goods and services purchased by households. The Consumer price index in the United States is defined by the Bureau of Labor Statistics as 'a measure of the average change over time in the prices paid by urban consumers for a market basket of consumer goods and services.' The Consumer price index is a statistical estimate constructed using the prices of a sample of representative items whose prices are collected periodically. Sub-indexes and sub-sub-indexes are computed for different categories and sub-categories of goods and services, being combined to produce the overall index with weights reflecting their shares in the total of the consumer expenditures covered by the index.
Deflation	In economics, deflation is a decrease in the general price level of goods and services. Deflation occurs when the inflation rate falls below 0% (a negative inflation rate). This should not be confused with disinflation, a slow-down in the inflation rate (i.e., when inflation declines to lower levels).

5. Monitoring Jobs and Inflation

CHAPTER HIGHLIGHTS & NOTES: KEY TERMS, PEOPLE, PLACES, CONCEPTS

Hyperinflation	In economics, hyperinflation occurs when a country experiences very high and usually accelerating rates of monetary and price inflation, causing the population to minimize their holdings of money. Under such conditions, the general price level within an economy increases rapidly as the official currency quickly loses real value. Meanwhile, the real value of economic items generally stay the same with respect to one another, and remain relatively stable in terms of foreign currencies.
Inflation	In economics, inflation is a sustained increase in the general price level of goods and services in an economy over a period of time. When the general price level rises, each unit of currency buys fewer goods and services. Consequently, inflation reflects a reduction in the purchasing power per unit of money - a loss of real value in the medium of exchange and unit of account within the economy.
Price level	The general price level is a hypothetical measure of overall prices for some set of goods and services, in a given region during a given interval, normalized relative to some base set. Typically, a price level is approximated with a price index.
Production	Production is a process of combining various material inputs and immaterial inputs in order to make something for consumption (the output). It is the act of creating output, a good or service which has value and contributes to the utility of individuals. Economic well-being is created in a production process, meaning all economic activities that aim directly or indirectly to satisfy human needs.
Consumer	A consumer is a person or group of people, such as a household, who are the final users of products or services. The consumer's use is final in the sense that the product is usually not improved by the use.
Price index	A price index is a normalized average of price relatives for a given class of goods or services in a given region, during a given interval of time. It is a statistic designed to help to compare how these price relatives, taken as a whole, differ between time periods or geographical locations. Price indexes have several potential uses.
Price	In ordinary usage, price is the quantity of payment or compensation given by one party to another in return for goods or services. In modern economies, prices are generally expressed in units of some form of currency. (For commodities, they are expressed as currency per unit weight of the commodity, e.g. euros per kilogram).
Purchasing power	Purchasing power is the number of goods or services that can be purchased with a unit of currency. For example, if one had taken one unit of currency to a store in the 1950s, it is probable that it would have been possible to buy a greater number of items than would today, indicating that one would have had a greater purchasing power in the 1950s.

5. Monitoring Jobs and Inflation

CHAPTER HIGHLIGHTS & NOTES: KEY TERMS, PEOPLE, PLACES, CONCEPTS

GDP deflator	In economics, the GDP deflator is a measure of the level of prices of all new, domestically produced, final goods and services in an economy. GDP stands for gross domestic product, the total value of all final goods and services produced within that economy during a specified period. Like the Consumer Price Index (CPI), the GDP deflator is a measure of price inflation/deflation with respect to a specific base year; the GDP deflator of the base year itself is equal to 100. Unlike the CPI, the GDP deflator is not based on a fixed basket of goods and services; the 'basket' for the GDP deflator is allowed to change from year to year with people's consumption and investment patterns.
Personal consumption	The Personal Consumption Expenditure measure is the component statistic for consumption in GDP collected by the BEA. It consists of the actual and imputed expenditures of households and includes data pertaining to durable and non-durable goods and services. It is essentially a measure of goods and services targeted towards individuals and consumed by individuals. The PCE price index (PCEPI), also referred to as the PCE deflator, PCE price deflator, or the Implicit Price Deflator for Personal Consumption Expenditures (IPD for PCE) by the BEA, and as the Chain-type Price Index for Personal Consumption Expenditures (CTPIPCE) by the FOMC, is a United States-wide indicator of the average increase in prices for all domestic personal consumption.
Deflator	In statistics, a deflator is a value that allows data to be measured over time in terms of some base period, usually through a price index, in order to distinguish between a changes in the money value of a gross national product that come from a change in prices, and changes from a change in physical output. It is the measure of the price level for some quantity. A deflator serves as a price index in which the effects of inflation are nulled.
Core inflation	Core inflation represents the long run trend in the price level. In measuring long run inflation, transitory price changes should be excluded. One way of accomplishing this is by excluding items frequently subject to volatile prices, like food and energy.
Inflationary gap	An inflationary gap, in economics, is the amount by which the actual gross domestic product exceeds potential full-employment GDP. It is one type of output gap, the other being a recessionary gap.
Macroeconomics	Macroeconomics is a branch of economics dealing with the performance, structure, behavior, and decision-making of an economy as a whole, rather than individual markets. This includes national, regional, and global economies. With microeconomics, macroeconomics is one of the two most general fields in economics.
Reserve	In financial accounting, the term reserve is most commonly used to describe any part of shareholders' equity, except for basic share capital.

5. Monitoring Jobs and Inflation

51

CHAPTER HIGHLIGHTS & NOTES: KEY TERMS, PEOPLE, PLACES, CONCEPTS

	In nonprofit accounting, an 'operating reserve' is commonly used to refer to unrestricted cash on hand available to sustain an organization, and nonprofit boards usually specify a target of maintaining several months of operating cash or a percentage of their annual income, called an Operating Reserve Ratio.
	Sometimes, reserve is used in the sense of the term provision; such a use, however, is inconsistent with the terminology suggested by International Accounting Standards Board.
Variable	In elementary mathematics, a variable is an alphabetic character representing a number which is either arbitrary or not fully specified or unknown. Making algebraic computations with variables as if they were explicit numbers allows one to solve a range of problems in a single computation. A typical example is the quadratic formula, which allows to solve every quadratic equation by simply substituting the numeric values of the coefficients of the given equation to the variables that represent them.

CHAPTER QUIZ: KEY TERMS, PEOPLE, PLACES, CONCEPTS

1. A _____ measures changes in the price level of a market basket of consumer goods and services purchased by households. The _____ in the United States is defined by the Bureau of Labor Statistics as 'a measure of the average change over time in the prices paid by urban consumers for a market basket of consumer goods and services.'

   The _____ is a statistical estimate constructed using the prices of a sample of representative items whose prices are collected periodically. Sub-indexes and sub-sub-indexes are computed for different categories and sub-categories of goods and services, being combined to produce the overall index with weights reflecting their shares in the total of the consumer expenditures covered by the index.

   a. Consumer price index
   b. Bad bank
   c. Bank failure
   d. Bundism

2. . The _____ Expenditure measure is the component statistic for consumption in GDP collected by the BEA. It consists of the actual and imputed expenditures of households and includes data pertaining to durable and non-durable goods and services. It is essentially a measure of goods and services targeted towards individuals and consumed by individuals.

   The PCE price index (PCEPI), also referred to as the PCE deflator, PCE price deflator, or the Implicit Price Deflator for _____ Expenditures (IPD for PCE) by the BEA, and as the Chain-type Price Index for _____ Expenditures (CTPIPCE) by the FOMC, is a United States-wide indicator of the average increase in prices for all domestic _____.

   a. Personal consumption

5. Monitoring Jobs and Inflation

CHAPTER QUIZ: KEY TERMS, PEOPLE, PLACES, CONCEPTS

   b. Hedonic index
   c. Higher Education Price Index
   d. Lipstick index

3. In mathematics, a _____ is a ratio between two measurements with different units. If the unit or quantity in respect of which something is changing is not specified, usually the _____ is per unit time. However, a _____ of change can be specified per unit time, or per unit of length or mass or another quantity.

   a. Bank rate
   b. Rate
   c. Cash accumulation equation
   d. Coupon leverage

4. An _____, in economics, is the amount by which the actual gross domestic product exceeds potential full-employment GDP. It is one type of output gap, the other being a recessionary gap.

   a. Base effect
   b. Inflationary gap
   c. Chronic inflation
   d. Core inflation

5. _____ occurs when people are without work and actively seeking work. The _____ rate is a measure of the prevalence of _____ and it is calculated as a percentage by dividing the number of unemployed individuals by all individuals currently in the labor force. During periods of recession, an economy usually experiences a relatively high _____ rate.

   a. Unemployment
   b. Bankruptcy
   c. Benefit shortfall
   d. Climate change

ANSWER KEY
5. Monitoring Jobs and Inflation

1. a
2. a
3. b
4. b
5. a

You can take the complete Online Interactive Chapter Practice Test

for 5. Monitoring Jobs and Inflation
on all key terms, persons, places, and concepts.

No Additional Costs

http://www.Cram101.com

Register, send an email request to Travis.Reese@Cram101.com to get your user Id and password.

Include your customer order number, and ISBN number from your studyguide Retailer.

6. Economic Growth

CHAPTER OUTLINE: KEY TERMS, PEOPLE, PLACES, CONCEPTS

	Business cycle
	Economic growth
	Real GDP
	World economy
	Demand
	Labor force
	Production possibilities frontier
	Supply
	Money
	Full employment
	Market
	Physical capital
	Human capital
	Loan
	Advance
	Productivity
	Technological change
	Diminishing returns
	Rate
	Returns
	Public good

6. Economic Growth
CHAPTER OUTLINE: KEY TERMS, PEOPLE, PLACES, CONCEPTS

	Saving
	International trade

CHAPTER HIGHLIGHTS & NOTES: KEY TERMS, PEOPLE, PLACES, CONCEPTS

Business cycle	The term business cycle refers to economy-wide fluctuations in production, trade and economic activity in general over several months or years in an economy organized on free-enterprise principles.
	The business cycle is the upward and downward movements of levels of GDP (gross domestic product) and refers to the period of expansions and contractions in the level of economic activities (business fluctuations) around its long-term growth trend.
	These fluctuations occur around a long-term growth trend, and typically involve shifts over time between periods of relatively rapid economic growth (an expansion or boom), and periods of relative stagnation or decline (a contraction or recession).
Economic growth	Economic growth is the increase in the market value of the goods and services produced by an economy over time. It is conventionally measured as the percent rate of increase in real gross domestic product, or real GDP. Of more importance is the growth of the ratio of GDP to population (GDP per capita), which is also called per capita income. An increase in per capita income is referred to as intensive growth.
Real GDP	Real Gross Domestic Product (real GDP) is a macroeconomic measure of the value of economic output adjusted for price changes . This adjustment transforms the money-value measure, nominal GDP, into an index for quantity of total output. GDP is the sum of consumer Spending, Investment made by industry, Excess of Exports over Imports and Government Spending.
World economy	The world economy, or global economy, generally refers to the economy, which is based on economies of all of the world's countries' national economies. Also global economy can be seen as the economy of global society and national economies - as economies of local societies, making the global one. It can be evaluated in various kind of ways.
Demand	In economics, demand for a good or service is an entire listing of the quantity of the good or service that a market would choose to buy, for every possible market price of the good or service.

6. Economic Growth

CHAPTER HIGHLIGHTS & NOTES: KEY TERMS, PEOPLE, PLACES, CONCEPTS

	(Note: This distinguishes 'demand' from 'quantity demanded', where demand is a listing or graphing of quantity demanded at each possible price. In contrast to demand, quantity demanded is the exact quantity demanded at a certain price.
Labor force	The labor force is the actual number of people available for work. The labor force of a country includes both the employed and the unemployed. The labor force participation rate, LFPR (or economic activity rate, EAR), is the ratio between the labor force and the overall size of their cohort (national population of the same age range).
Production possibilities frontier	In economics, a production-possibility frontier, sometimes called a production-possibility curve, production-possibility boundary or product transformation curve, is a graph that shows the various combinations of amounts that two commodities could produce using the same fixed total amount of each of the factors of production. Graphically bounding the production set for fixed input quantities, the production possibilities frontier curve shows the maximum possible production level of one commodity for any given production level of the other, given the existing state of technology. By doing so, it defines productive efficiency in the context of that production set: a point on the frontier indicates efficient use of the available inputs, while a point beneath the curve indicates inefficiency.
Supply	In economics, supply refers to the amount of a product that producers and firms are willing to sell at a given price all other factors being held constant. Usually, supply is plotted as a supply curve showing the relationship of price to the amount of product businesses are willing to sell.
Money	Monetary disequilibrium theory is basically a product of the Monetarist school mainly represented in the works of Leland Yeager and Austrian macroeconomics. The basic concept of monetary equilibrium (disequilibrium) was, however, defined in terms of an individual's demand for cash balance by Mises (1912) in his Theory of Money and Credit. Monetary Disequilibrium is one of three theories of macroeconomic fluctuations which accord an important role to money, the others being the Austrian theory of the business cycle and one based on rational expectations.
Full employment	Full employment, in macroeconomics, is the level of employment rates where there is no cyclical or deficient-demand unemployment. It is defined by the majority of mainstream economists as being an acceptable level of unemployment somewhere above 0%. The discrepancy from 0% arises due to non-cyclical types of unemployment.
Market	A financial market is a market in which people and entities can trade financial securities, commodities, and other fungible items of value at low transaction costs and at prices that reflect supply and demand. Securities include stocks and bonds, and commodities include precious metals or agricultural goods.

6. Economic Growth

CHAPTER HIGHLIGHTS & NOTES: KEY TERMS, PEOPLE, PLACES, CONCEPTS

Physical capital	In economics, physical capital or just 'capital' refers to a factor of production, such as machinery, buildings, or computers. The production function takes the general form Y=f(K, L), where Y is output, K is capital stock and L is labor. In economic theory, physical capital is one of the three primary factors of production, also known as inputs production function.
Human capital	Human capital is the stock of competencies, knowledge, habits, social and personality attributes, including creativity, cognitive abilities, embodied in the ability to perform labor so as to produce economic value. It is an aggregate economic view of the human being acting within economies, which is an attempt to capture the social, biological, cultural and psychological complexity as they interact in explicit and/or economic transactions. Many theories explicitly connect investment in human capital development to education, and the role of human capital in economic development, productivity growth, and innovation has frequently been cited as a justification for government subsidies for education and job skills training.
Loan	An introductory rate is an interest rate charged to a customer during the initial stages of a loan. The rate, which can be as low as 0%, is not permanent and after it expires a normal or higher than normal rate will apply. The purpose of the introductory rate is to market the loan to customers and to seem attractive.
Advance	Advance is a certified, independent trade union affiliated to the TUC representing workers within the bank Santander UK, the UK subsidiary of Santander Group. The union was formerly known as The Abbey National Group Union (ANGU) before it expanded to include staff of Alliance & Leicester and Bradford & Bingley following their acquisitions by Santander. Its aims are the supporting and representing its members in all aspects of their employment.
Productivity	Productivity is the ratio of output to inputs in production; it is an average measure of the efficiency of production. Efficiency of production means production's capability to create incomes which is measured by the formula real output value minus real input value. Increasing national productivity can raise living standards because more real income improves people's ability to purchase goods and services, enjoy leisure, improve housing and education and contribute to social and environmental programs.
Technological change	Technological change, technological development, technological achievement, or technological progress is the overall process of invention, innovation and diffusion of technology or processes. In essence technological change is the invention of technologies (including processes) and their commercialization via research and development (producing emerging technologies), the continual improvement of technologies (in which they often become less expensive), and the diffusion of technologies throughout industry or society (which sometimes involves disruption and convergence). In short, technological change is based on both better and more technology.

6. Economic Growth

CHAPTER HIGHLIGHTS & NOTES: KEY TERMS, PEOPLE, PLACES, CONCEPTS

Diminishing returns	In economics, diminishing returns is the decrease in the marginal (per-unit) output of a production process as the amount of a single factor of production is increased, while the amounts of all other factors of production stay constant. The law of diminishing returns states that in all productive processes, adding more of one factor of production, while holding all others constant ('ceteris paribus'), will at some point yield lower per-unit returns. The law of diminishing returns does not imply that adding more of a factor will decrease the total production, a condition known as negative returns, though in fact this is common.
Rate	In mathematics, a rate is a ratio between two measurements with different units. If the unit or quantity in respect of which something is changing is not specified, usually the rate is per unit time. However, a rate of change can be specified per unit time, or per unit of length or mass or another quantity.
Returns	Returns, in economics and political economy, are the distributions or payments awarded to the various suppliers of the factors of production.
Public good	In economics, a public good is a good that is both non-excludable and non-rivalrous in that individuals cannot be effectively excluded from use and where use by one individual does not reduce availability to others. Examples of public goods include fresh air, knowledge, lighthouses, national defense, flood control systems and street lighting. Public goods that are available everywhere are sometimes referred to as global public goods.
Saving	Saving is income not spent, or deferred consumption. Methods of saving include putting money aside in a bank or pension plan. Saving also includes reducing expenditures, such as recurring costs.
International trade	International trade is the exchange of capital, goods, and services across international borders or territories. In most countries, such trade represents a significant share of gross domestic product (GDP). While international trade has been present throughout much of history, its economic, social, and political importance has been on the rise in recent centuries.

6. Economic Growth

CHAPTER QUIZ: KEY TERMS, PEOPLE, PLACES, CONCEPTS

1. _____ is income not spent, or deferred consumption. Methods of _____ include putting money aside in a bank or pension plan. _____ also includes reducing expenditures, such as recurring costs.

   a. Federal Reserve
   b. Fuel protests in the United Kingdom
   c. Saving
   d. Bankruptcy tourism

2. In economics, _____ for a good or service is an entire listing of the quantity of the good or service that a market would choose to buy, for every possible market price of the good or service. (Note: This distinguishes '_____' from 'quantity demanded', where _____ is a listing or graphing of quantity demanded at each possible price. In contrast to _____, quantity demanded is the exact quantity demanded at a certain price.

   a. Bad bank
   b. Demand
   c. Bundism
   d. Communist Bund

3. In economics, _____ or just 'capital' refers to a factor of production, such as machinery, buildings, or computers. The production function takes the general form Y=f(K, L), where Y is output, K is capital stock and L is labor. In economic theory, _____ is one of the three primary factors of production, also known as inputs production function.

   a. quantity theory
   b. production possibilities frontier
   c. quantity theory of money
   d. Physical capital

4. In economics, _____ is the decrease in the marginal (per-unit) output of a production process as the amount of a single factor of production is increased, while the amounts of all other factors of production stay constant.

   The law of _____ states that in all productive processes, adding more of one factor of production, while holding all others constant ('ceteris paribus'), will at some point yield lower per-unit returns. The law of _____ does not imply that adding more of a factor will decrease the total production, a condition known as negative returns, though in fact this is common.

   a. law of supply
   b. Federal Reserve
   c. Diminishing returns
   d. 2010 student protest in Dublin

5. . The term _____ refers to economy-wide fluctuations in production, trade and economic activity in general over several months or years in an economy organized on free-enterprise principles.

6. Economic Growth

CHAPTER QUIZ: KEY TERMS, PEOPLE, PLACES, CONCEPTS

The _____ is the upward and downward movements of levels of GDP (gross domestic product) and refers to the period of expansions and contractions in the level of economic activities (business fluctuations) around its long-term growth trend.

These fluctuations occur around a long-term growth trend, and typically involve shifts over time between periods of relatively rapid economic growth (an expansion or boom), and periods of relative stagnation or decline (a contraction or recession).

a. Business cycle
b. Bank failure
c. Jewish Social Democratic Party
d. Communist Bund

ANSWER KEY
6. Economic Growth

1. c
2. b
3. d
4. c
5. a

You can take the complete Online Interactive Chapter Practice Test

for 6. Economic Growth
on all key terms, persons, places, and concepts.

No Additional Costs

http://www.Cram101.com

Register, send an email request to Travis.Reese@Cram101.com to get your user Id and password.

Include your customer order number, and ISBN number from your studyguide Retailer.

7. Finance, Saving, and Investment

CHAPTER OUTLINE: KEY TERMS, PEOPLE, PLACES, CONCEPTS

	Finance
	Financial capital
	Financial market
	Human capital
	Net investment
	Physical capital
	Saving
	Wealth
	Capital
	Gros
	Bond
	Bond market
	Mortgage-backed security
	Commercial bank
	Credit
	Financial crisis
	Good
	JPMorgan Chase
	Lehman Brothers
	Merrill Lynch
	Stock

7. Finance, Saving, and Investment
CHAPTER OUTLINE: KEY TERMS, PEOPLE, PLACES, CONCEPTS

_____	Stock market
_____	Consumer Financial Protection Bureau
_____	Financial Stability Oversight Council
_____	Federal Reserve
_____	Federal Reserve System
_____	Financial asset
_____	Insolvency
_____	Interest rate
_____	Net worth
_____	Price level
_____	Asset
_____	Price
_____	Loanable funds
_____	Nominal interest rate
_____	Real interest rate
_____	Demand
_____	Quantitative easing
_____	Supply
_____	Money
_____	Index
_____	Budget surplus

7. Finance, Saving, and Investment

CHAPTER OUTLINE: KEY TERMS, PEOPLE, PLACES, CONCEPTS

Government budget

CHAPTER HIGHLIGHTS & NOTES: KEY TERMS, PEOPLE, PLACES, CONCEPTS

Finance	Finance is a field within economics that deals with the allocation of assets and liabilities over time under conditions of certainty and uncertainty. Finance can also be defined as the science of money management. A key point in finance is the time value of money, which states that one unit of currency today is worth more than one unit of currency tomorrow.
Financial capital	Financial capital is any economic resource measured in terms of money used by entrepreneurs and businesses to buy what they need to make their products or to provide their services to the sector of the economy upon which their operation is based, i.e. retail, corporate, investment banking, etc.
Financial market	A financial market is a market in which people and entities can trade financial securities, commodities, and other fungible items of value at low transaction costs and at prices that reflect supply and demand. Securities include stocks and bonds, and commodities include precious metals or agricultural goods. There are both general markets (where many commodities are traded) and specialized markets (where only one commodity is traded).
Human capital	Human capital is the stock of competencies, knowledge, habits, social and personality attributes, including creativity, cognitive abilities, embodied in the ability to perform labor so as to produce economic value. It is an aggregate economic view of the human being acting within economies, which is an attempt to capture the social, biological, cultural and psychological complexity as they interact in explicit and/or economic transactions. Many theories explicitly connect investment in human capital development to education, and the role of human capital in economic development, productivity growth, and innovation has frequently been cited as a justification for government subsidies for education and job skills training.
Net investment	In economics, net investment refers to an activity of spending which increases the availability of fixed capital goods or means of production. It is the total spending on new fixed investment minus replacement investment, which simply replaces depreciated capital goods. Net Investment is equal to the Gross investment minus depreciation

7. Finance, Saving, and Investment

CHAPTER HIGHLIGHTS & NOTES: KEY TERMS, PEOPLE, PLACES, CONCEPTS

Physical capital	In economics, physical capital or just 'capital' refers to a factor of production, such as machinery, buildings, or computers. The production function takes the general form $Y=f(K, L)$, where Y is output, K is capital stock and L is labor. In economic theory, physical capital is one of the three primary factors of production, also known as inputs production function.
Saving	Saving is income not spent, or deferred consumption. Methods of saving include putting money aside in a bank or pension plan. Saving also includes reducing expenditures, such as recurring costs.
Wealth	The modern understanding of Wealth is the abundance of valuable resources or material possessions. This excludes the core meaning as held in the originating old English word weal, which is from an Indo-European word stem. In this larger understanding of wealth, an individual, community, region or country that possesses an abundance of such possessions or resources to the benefit of the common good is known as wealthy.
Capital	In economics, capital goods, real capital, or capital assets are already-produced durable goods or any non-financial asset that is used in production of goods or services. Capital goods are not significantly consumed in the production process though they may depreciate. How a capital good or is maintained or returned to its pre-production state varies with the type of capital involved.
Gros	A gros was a type of silver coinage of France from the time of Saint Louis. There were gros tournois and gros parisis. The gros was sub-divided in half gros and quarter gros.
Bond	In finance, a bond is an instrument of indebtedness of the bond issuer to the holders. It is a debt security, under which the issuer owes the holders a debt and, depending on the terms of the bond, is obliged to pay them interest (the coupon) and/or to repay the principal at a later date, termed the maturity date. Interest is usually payable at fixed intervals (semiannual, annual, sometimes monthly).
Bond market	The bond market is a financial market where participants can issue new debt, known as the primary market, or buy and sell debt securities, known as the secondary market. This is usually in the form of bonds, but it may include notes, bills, and so on. The primary goal of the bond market is to provide a mechanism for long term funding of public and private expenditures.
Mortgage-backed security	A mortgage-backed security is a type of asset-backed security that is secured by a mortgage, or more commonly a collection ('pool') of sometimes hundreds of mortgages. The mortgages are sold to a group of individuals (a government agency or investment bank) that 'securitizes', or packages, the loans together into a security that can be sold to investors.

7. Finance, Saving, and Investment

CHAPTER HIGHLIGHTS & NOTES: KEY TERMS, PEOPLE, PLACES, CONCEPTS

Commercial bank	A commercial bank is a type of bank that provides services such as accepting deposits, making business loans, and offering basic investment products.
	Commercial bank can also refer to a bank or a division of a bank that mostly deals with deposits and loans from corporations or large businesses, as opposed to individual members of the public .
	In the US the term commercial bank was often used to distinguish it from an investment bank due to differences in bank regulation.
Credit	Credit is the trust which allows one party to provide resources to another party where that second party does not reimburse the first party immediately (thereby generating a debt), but instead arranges either to repay or return those resources (or other materials of equal value) at a later date. The resources provided may be financial (e.g. granting a loan), or they may consist of goods or services (e.g. consumer credit). Credit encompasses any form of deferred payment.
Financial crisis	The term financial crisis is applied broadly to a variety of situations in which some financial assets suddenly lose a large part of their nominal value. In the 19th and early 20th centuries, many financial crises were associated with banking panics, and many recessions coincided with these panics. Other situations that are often called financial crises include stock market crashes and the bursting of other financial bubbles, currency crises, and sovereign defaults.
Good	In economics, a good is a material that satisfies human wants and provides utility, for example, to a consumer making a purchase. A common distinction is made between 'goods' that are tangible property (also called goods) and services, which are non-physical. Commodities may be used as a synonym for economic goods but often refer to marketable raw materials and primary products.
JPMorgan Chase	JPMorgan Chase & Co. is an American multinational banking and financial services holding company. It is the largest bank in the United States, with total assets of US$2.415 trillion. It is a major provider of financial services, and according to Forbes magazine is the world's third largest public company based on a composite ranking.
Lehman Brothers	Lehman Brothers Holdings Inc. (former NYSE ticker symbol LEH) was a global financial services firm. Before declaring bankruptcy in 2008, Lehman was the fourth-largest investment bank in the US (behind Goldman Sachs, Morgan Stanley, and Merrill Lynch), doing business in investment banking, equity and fixed-income sales and trading (especially U.S. Treasury securities), research, investment management, private equity, and private banking.
Merrill Lynch	Merrill Lynch Wealth Management is the wealth management division of Bank of America. It is headquartered in New York City, and occupies the entire 34 stories of the Four World Financial Center building in Manhattan. With over 15,000 financial advisors and $2.2 trillion in client assets, it is the world's largest brokerage. It has its origins in Merrill Lynch & Co., Inc., which prior to 2009 was publicly owned and traded on the New York Stock Exchange under the ticker symbol MER.

7. Finance, Saving, and Investment

CHAPTER HIGHLIGHTS & NOTES: KEY TERMS, PEOPLE, PLACES, CONCEPTS

	Merrill Lynch & Co. agreed to be acquired by Bank of America on September 14, 2008, at the height of the 2008 Financial Crisis.
Stock	The stock of a corporation constitutes the equity stake of its owners. It represents the residual assets of the company that would be due to stockholders after discharge of all senior claims such as secured and unsecured debt. Stockholders' equity cannot be withdrawn from the company in a way that is intended to be detrimental to the company's creditors.
Stock market	A stock market or equity market is the aggregation of buyers and sellers of stocks (shares); these are securities listed on a stock exchange as well as those only traded privately.
Consumer Financial Protection Bureau	The Consumer Financial Protection Bureau is an independent agency of the United States government responsible for consumer protection in the financial sector. Its jurisdiction includes banks, credit unions, securities firms, payday lenders, mortgage-servicing operations, foreclosure relief services, debt collectors and other financial companies operating in the United States. The Consumer Financial Protection Bureau's creation was authorized by the Dodd-Frank Wall Street Reform and Consumer Protection Act, whose passage in 2010 was a legislative response to the financial crisis of 2007-08 and the subsequent Great Recession.
Financial Stability Oversight Council	The Financial Stability Oversight Council is a United States federal government organization, established by Title I of the Dodd-Frank Wall Street Reform and Consumer Protection Act, which was signed into law by President Barack Obama on July 21, 2010. The Dodd-Frank Act provides the Council with broad authorities to identify and monitor excessive risks to the U.S. financial system arising from the distress or failure of large, interconnected bank holding companies or non-bank financial companies, or from risks that could arise outside the financial system; to eliminate expectations that any American financial firm is 'too big to fail'; and to respond to emerging threats to U.S. financial stability. The Act also designates the Secretary of the Treasury as Chairperson. Inherent to the Financial Stability Oversight Council's role as a consultative council is facilitation of communication among financial regulators.
Federal Reserve	The Federal Reserve System (also known as the Federal Reserve, and informally as the Fed) is the central banking system of the United States. It was created on December 23, 1913, with the enactment of the Federal Reserve Act, largely in response to a series of financial panics, particularly a severe panic in 1907. Over time, the roles and responsibilities of the Federal Reserve System have expanded, and its structure has evolved. Events such as the Great Depression were major factors leading to changes in the system.
Federal Reserve System	The Federal Reserve System is the central banking system of the United States. It was created on December 23, 1913, with the enactment of the Federal Reserve Act, largely in response to a series of financial panics, particularly a severe panic in 1907. Over time, the roles and responsibilities of the Federal Reserve System have expanded, and its structure has evolved.

7. Finance, Saving, and Investment

CHAPTER HIGHLIGHTS & NOTES: KEY TERMS, PEOPLE, PLACES, CONCEPTS

Financial asset	A financial asset is an intangible asset that derives value because of a contractual claim. Examples include bank deposits, bonds, and stocks. Financial assets are usually more liquid than tangible assets, such as land or real estate, and are traded on financial markets.
Insolvency	Insolvency is the inability of a debtor to pay their debt. In many sources, the definition also includes the phrase 'or the state of having liabilities that exceed assets' or some similar phrase.
	Cash flow insolvency involves a lack of liquidity to pay debts as they fall due.
Interest rate	An interest rate is the rate at which interest is paid by a borrower for the use of money that they borrow from a lender (creditor). Specifically, the interest rate is a percent of principal (P) paid a certain amount of times (m) per period (usually quoted per annum). For example, a small company borrows capital from a bank to buy new assets for its business, and in return the lender receives interest at a predetermined interest rate for deferring the use of funds and instead lending it to the borrower.
Net worth	In business, net worth is the total assets minus total outside liabilities of an individual or a company. Put another way, net worth is what is owned minus what is owed. For a company, this is called shareholders' preference and may be referred to as book value.
Price level	The general price level is a hypothetical measure of overall prices for some set of goods and services, in a given region during a given interval, normalized relative to some base set. Typically, a price level is approximated with a price index.
Asset	An 'asset' in economic theory is an output good which can only be partially consumed or input as a factor of production (like a cement mixer) which can only be partially used up in production. The necessary quality for an asset is that value remains after the period of analysis so it can be used as a store of value. As such, financial instruments like corporate bonds and common stocks are assets because they store value for the next period.
Price	In ordinary usage, price is the quantity of payment or compensation given by one party to another in return for goods or services.
	In modern economies, prices are generally expressed in units of some form of currency. (For commodities, they are expressed as currency per unit weight of the commodity, e.g. euros per kilogram).
Loanable funds	In economics, the loanable funds market is a hypothetical market that brings savers and borrowers together, also bringing together the money available in commercial banks and lending institutions available for firms and households to finance expenditures, either investments or consumption. Savers supply the loanable funds; for instance, buying bonds will transfer their money to the institution issuing the bond, which can be a firm or government.

7. Finance, Saving, and Investment

CHAPTER HIGHLIGHTS & NOTES: KEY TERMS, PEOPLE, PLACES, CONCEPTS

Nominal interest rate	In finance and economics, nominal interest rate or nominal rate of interest refers to two distinct things: the rate of interest before adjustment for inflation ; or, for interest rates 'as stated' without adjustment for the full effect of compounding (also referred to as the nominal annual rate). An interest rate is called nominal if the frequency of compounding (e.g. a month) is not identical to the basic time unit (normally a year).
Real interest rate	The real interest rate is the rate of interest an investor expects to receive after allowing for inflation. It can be described more formally by the Fisher equation, which states that the real interest rate is approximately the nominal interest rate minus the inflation rate. If, for example, an investor were able to lock in a 5% interest rate for the coming year and anticipated a 2% rise in prices, they would expect to earn a real interest rate of 3%.
Demand	In economics, demand for a good or service is an entire listing of the quantity of the good or service that a market would choose to buy, for every possible market price of the good or service. (Note: This distinguishes 'demand' from 'quantity demanded', where demand is a listing or graphing of quantity demanded at each possible price. In contrast to demand, quantity demanded is the exact quantity demanded at a certain price.
Quantitative easing	Quantitative easing is an unconventional monetary policy used by central banks to stimulate the economy when standard monetary policy has become ineffective. A central bank implements quantitative easing by buying specified amounts of financial assets from commercial banks and other private institutions, thus raising the prices of those financial assets and lowering their yield, while simultaneously increasing the monetary base. This is distinguished from the more usual policy of buying or selling short term government bonds in order to keep interbank interest rates at a specified target value.
Supply	In economics, supply refers to the amount of a product that producers and firms are willing to sell at a given price all other factors being held constant. Usually, supply is plotted as a supply curve showing the relationship of price to the amount of product businesses are willing to sell.
Money	Monetary disequilibrium theory is basically a product of the Monetarist school mainly represented in the works of Leland Yeager and Austrian macroeconomics. The basic concept of monetary equilibrium (disequilibrium) was, however, defined in terms of an individual's demand for cash balance by Mises (1912) in his Theory of Money and Credit. Monetary Disequilibrium is one of three theories of macroeconomic fluctuations which accord an important role to money, the others being the Austrian theory of the business cycle and one based on rational expectations.
Index	In economics and finance, an index is a statistical measure of changes in a representative group of individual data points. These data may be derived from any number of sources, including company performance, prices, productivity, and employment.

7. Finance, Saving, and Investment

CHAPTER HIGHLIGHTS & NOTES: KEY TERMS, PEOPLE, PLACES, CONCEPTS

Budget surplus	A government budget is a government document presenting the government's proposed revenues and spending for a financial year. The government budget balance, also alternatively referred to as general government balance, public budget balance, or public fiscal balance, is the overall difference between government revenues and spending. A positive balance is called a government budget surplus, and a negative balance is a government budget deficit.
Government budget	A government budget is a government document presenting the government's proposed revenues and spending for a financial year that is often passed by the legislature, approved by the chief executive or president and presented by the Finance Minister to the nation. The budget is also known as the Annual Financial Statement of the country. This document estimates the anticipated government revenues and government expenditures for the ensuing (current) financial year.

CHAPTER QUIZ: KEY TERMS, PEOPLE, PLACES, CONCEPTS

1. In economics, _____ or just 'capital' refers to a factor of production, such as machinery, buildings, or computers. The production function takes the general form Y=f(K, L), where Y is output, K is capital stock and L is labor. In economic theory, _____ is one of the three primary factors of production, also known as inputs production function.

    a. quantity theory
    b. Physical capital
    c. quantity theory of money
    d. comparative advantage

2. _____ & Co. is an American multinational banking and financial services holding company. It is the largest bank in the United States, with total assets of US$2.415 trillion. It is a major provider of financial services, and according to Forbes magazine is the world's third largest public company based on a composite ranking.

    a. JPMorgan Chase
    b. Bank of America Merrill Lynch
    c. Barclays Investment Bank
    d. BNP Paribas CIB

3. . _____ is income not spent, or deferred consumption. Methods of _____ include putting money aside in a bank or pension plan. _____ also includes reducing expenditures, such as recurring costs.

    a. Federal Reserve
    b. Fuel protests in the United Kingdom
    c. 2010 student protest in Dublin

7. Finance, Saving, and Investment

CHAPTER QUIZ: KEY TERMS, PEOPLE, PLACES, CONCEPTS

4. A _____ is a market in which people and entities can trade financial securities, commodities, and other fungible items of value at low transaction costs and at prices that reflect supply and demand. Securities include stocks and bonds, and commodities include precious metals or agricultural goods.

    There are both general markets (where many commodities are traded) and specialized markets (where only one commodity is traded).

    a. Bad bank
    b. Bank failure
    c. Bank code
    d. Financial market

5. In economics, _____ for a good or service is an entire listing of the quantity of the good or service that a market would choose to buy, for every possible market price of the good or service. (Note: This distinguishes '_____' from 'quantity demanded', where _____ is a listing or graphing of quantity demanded at each possible price. In contrast to _____, quantity demanded is the exact quantity demanded at a certain price.

    a. Bad bank
    b. Bank failure
    c. Demand
    d. Communist Bund

ANSWER KEY
7. Finance, Saving, and Investment

1. b
2. a
3. d
4. d
5. c

You can take the complete Online Interactive Chapter Practice Test

for 7. Finance, Saving, and Investment
on all key terms, persons, places, and concepts.

No Additional Costs

http://www.Cram101.com

Register, send an email request to Travis.Reese@Cram101.com to get your user Id and password.

Include your customer order number, and ISBN number from your studyguide Retailer.

8. Money, the Price Level, and Inflation

CHAPTER OUTLINE: KEY TERMS, PEOPLE, PLACES, CONCEPTS

	Barter
	Double coincidence
	Mean
	Medium of exchange
	Money
	Unit of account
	Coincidence
	Currency
	Deposit
	Store of value
	Multiplier
	Credit card
	Bank
	Bank of America
	Citigroup
	Commercial bank
	Credit union
	Depository institution
	Federal funds
	Federal funds rate
	JPMorgan Chase

8. Money, the Price Level, and Inflation
CHAPTER OUTLINE: KEY TERMS, PEOPLE, PLACES, CONCEPTS

- Money market
- Mutual fund
- Reserve
- Cash
- Saving
- Savings bank
- Deposit insurance
- Federal Deposit Insurance Corporation
- Loan
- Base period
- Reserve banking
- Federal Reserve
- Financial innovation
- Innovation
- Lehman Brothers
- Bank reserves
- Federal Open Market Committee
- Federal Reserve Bank
- Federal Reserve System
- Monetary policy
- Open market

8. Money, the Price Level, and Inflation

CHAPTER OUTLINE: KEY TERMS, PEOPLE, PLACES, CONCEPTS

- Arbitrage
- Balance sheet
- Monetary base
- Mortgage-backed security
- Open market operation
- Asset
- Financial crisis
- Recession
- Lender of last resort
- Excess reserves
- Money creation
- Money multiplier
- Quantitative easing
- Interest rate
- Nominal interest rate
- Nominal money
- Price
- Price level
- Real GDP
- Demand
- Demand for money

8. Money, the Price Level, and Inflation
CHAPTER OUTLINE: KEY TERMS, PEOPLE, PLACES, CONCEPTS

	Supply
	Money supply
	Short run
	Quantity theory
	Exchange
	Inflation
	Interest
	Rate
	Reserve ratio

CHAPTER HIGHLIGHTS & NOTES: KEY TERMS, PEOPLE, PLACES, CONCEPTS

Barter	Barter is a system of exchange where goods or services are directly exchanged for other goods or services without using a medium of exchange, such as money. It is distinguishable from gift economies in many ways; one of them is that the reciprocal exchange is immediate and not delayed in time. It is usually bilateral, but may be multilateral (i.e., mediated through barter organizations) and, in most developed countries, usually only exists parallel to monetary systems to a very limited extent.
Double coincidence	The coincidence of wants problem (often 'double coincidence of wants') is the situation where the supplier of good A wants good B and the supplier of good B wants good A It is an important category of transaction costs that impose severe limitations on economies lacking a medium of exchange, which have to rely on barter or other in-kind transactions. The problem is caused by the improbability of the wants, needs, or events that cause or motivate a transaction occurring at the same time and the same place. One example is the bar musician who is 'paid' with liquor or food, items which his landlord will not accept as rent payment, when the musician would rather have a month's shelter.

8. Money, the Price Level, and Inflation

CHAPTER HIGHLIGHTS & NOTES: KEY TERMS, PEOPLE, PLACES, CONCEPTS

Mean	In mathematics, mean has several different definitions depending on the context.
	In probability and statistics, mean and expected value are used synonymously to refer to one measure of the central tendency either of a probability distribution or of the random variable characterized by that distribution. In the case of a discrete probability distribution of a random variable X, the mean is equal to the sum over every possible value weighted by the probability of that value; that is, it is computed by taking the product of each possible value x of X and its probability P(x), and then adding all these products together, giving $\mu = \sum xP(x)$.
Medium of exchange	A medium of exchange is an intermediary used in trade to avoid the inconveniences of a pure barter system.
	By contrast, as William Stanley Jevons argued, in a barter system there must be a coincidence of wants before two people can trade - one must want exactly what the other has to offer, when and where it is offered, so that the exchange can occur. A medium of exchange permits the value of goods to be assessed and rendered in terms of the intermediary, most often, a form of money widely accepted to buy any other good.
Money	Monetary disequilibrium theory is basically a product of the Monetarist school mainly represented in the works of Leland Yeager and Austrian macroeconomics. The basic concept of monetary equilibrium (disequilibrium) was, however, defined in terms of an individual's demand for cash balance by Mises (1912) in his Theory of Money and Credit.
	Monetary Disequilibrium is one of three theories of macroeconomic fluctuations which accord an important role to money, the others being the Austrian theory of the business cycle and one based on rational expectations.
Unit of account	The Unidad de Fomento is a Unit of account that is used in Chile. The exchange rate between the UF and the Chilean peso is now (today) constantly adjusted to inflation so that the value of the Unidad de Fomento remains constant on a daily basis during low inflation.
	It was created on January 20, 1968, for the use in determining principal (monetary item) and interest (constant real value non-monetary item) in international secured loans (monetary items) for development, subject to revaluation according to the variations of inflation.
Coincidence	A coincidence is a remarkable concurrence of events or circumstances which have no apparent causal connection with each other. The perception of remarkable coincidences may lead to supernatural, occult, or paranormal claims. Or it may lead to belief in fatalism, which is a doctrine that events will happen in the exact manner of a predetermined plan.
Currency	A currency in the most specific use of the word refers to money in any form when in actual use or circulation, as a medium of exchange, especially circulating paper money.

8. Money, the Price Level, and Inflation

CHAPTER HIGHLIGHTS & NOTES: KEY TERMS, PEOPLE, PLACES, CONCEPTS

	This use is synonymous with banknotes, or (sometimes) with banknotes plus coins, meaning the physical tokens used for money by a government. A much more general use of the word currency is anything that is used in any circumstances, as a medium of exchange.
Deposit	Individuals and corporations need money to pursue their daily business. They place the money on deposit to earn interest, using the money market. Types of deposits are:•Transactional account (checking account or current account, by country), the depositor has the right to use the money at any time, sometimes short notice periods are agreed; also called call deposit or sight deposit•Term deposit bear a fixed time and fixed interest rate•Fixed deposit in India•Overnight lending occurs usually from noon to noon, using a special rate.
Store of value	A store of value is the function of an asset that can be saved, retrieved and exchanged at a later time, and be predictably useful when retrieved. The most common store of value in modern times has been money, currency, or a commodity like gold, or financial capital. The point of any store of value is intrinsic risk management due to an inherent stable demand for the underlying asset.
Multiplier	In economics, a multiplier is a factor of proportionality that measures how much an endogenous variable changes in response to a change in some exogenous variable. For example, suppose variable x changes by 1 unit, which causes another variable y to change by M units. Then the multiplier is M.
Credit card	A credit card is a payment card issued to users as a system of payment. It allows the cardholder to pay for goods and services based on the holder's promise to pay for them. The issuer of the card creates a revolving account and grants a line of credit to the consumer (or the user) from which the user can borrow money for payment to a merchant or as a cash advance to the user.
Bank	A bank is a financial institution and a financial intermediary that accepts deposits and channels those deposits into lending activities, either directly by loaning or indirectly through capital markets. A bank links together customers that have capital deficits and customers with capital surpluses. Due to their influential status within the financial system and upon national economies, banks are highly regulated in most countries.
Bank of America	The Bank of America Corporation is an American multinational banking and financial services corporation headquartered in Charlotte, North Carolina. It is the second largest bank holding company in the United States by assets. As of 2010, Bank of America is the fifth-largest company in the United States by total revenue, and the third-largest non-oil company in the U.S. (after Walmart and General Electric).

8. Money, the Price Level, and Inflation

CHAPTER HIGHLIGHTS & NOTES: KEY TERMS, PEOPLE, PLACES, CONCEPTS

Citigroup	Citigroup Inc. or Citi is an American multinational financial services corporation headquartered in Manhattan, New York City. Citigroup was formed from one of the world's largest mergers in history by combining the banking giant Citicorp and financial conglomerate Travelers Group in October 1998 (announced on April 7, 1998).
Commercial bank	A commercial bank is a type of bank that provides services such as accepting deposits, making business loans, and offering basic investment products. Commercial bank can also refer to a bank or a division of a bank that mostly deals with deposits and loans from corporations or large businesses, as opposed to individual members of the public. In the US the term commercial bank was often used to distinguish it from an investment bank due to differences in bank regulation.
Credit union	A credit union is a member-owned financial cooperative, democratically controlled by its members, and operated for the purpose of promoting thrift, providing credit at competitive rates, and providing other financial services to its members. Many credit unions also provide services intended to support community development or sustainable international development on a local level. Worldwide, credit union systems vary significantly in terms of total system assets and average institution asset size, ranging from volunteer operations with a handful of members to institutions with assets worth several billion US dollars and hundreds of thousands of members.
Depository institution	A depository institution is a financial institution in the United States that is legally allowed to accept monetary deposits from consumers. Federal depository institutions are regulated by the Federal Deposit Insurance Corporation (FDIC). An example of a non-depository institution might be a mortgage bank.
Federal funds	In the United States, federal funds are overnight borrowings between banks and other entities to maintain their bank reserves at the Federal Reserve. Banks keep reserves at Federal Reserve Banks to meet their reserve requirements and to clear financial transactions. Transactions in the federal funds market enable depository institutions with reserve balances in excess of reserve requirements to lend reserves to institutions with reserve deficiencies.
Federal funds rate	In the United States, the federal funds rate is the interest rate at which depository institutions actively trade balances held at the Federal Reserve, called federal funds, with each other, usually overnight, on an uncollateralized basis. Institutions with surplus balances in their accounts lend those balances to institutions in need of larger balances. The federal funds rate is an important benchmark in financial markets.
JPMorgan Chase	JPMorgan Chase & Co.

8. Money, the Price Level, and Inflation

CHAPTER HIGHLIGHTS & NOTES: KEY TERMS, PEOPLE, PLACES, CONCEPTS

	is an American multinational banking and financial services holding company. It is the largest bank in the United States, with total assets of US$2.415 trillion. It is a major provider of financial services, and according to Forbes magazine is the world's third largest public company based on a composite ranking.
Money market	As money became a commodity, the money market became a component of the financial markets for assets involved in short-term borrowing, lending, buying and selling with original maturities of one year or less. Trading in the money markets is done over the counter and is wholesale. Various instruments exist, such as Treasury bills, commercial paper, bankers' acceptances, deposits, certificates of deposit, bills of exchange, repurchase agreements, federal funds, and short-lived mortgage-, and asset-backed securities.
Mutual fund	A mutual fund is a type of professionally managed collective investment scheme that pools money from many investors to purchase securities. While there is no legal definition of the term 'mutual fund', it is most commonly applied only to those collective investment vehicles that are regulated and sold to the general public. They are sometimes referred to as 'investment companies' or 'registered investment companies.' Most mutual funds are 'open-ended,' meaning stockholders can buy or sell shares of the fund at any time.
Reserve	In financial accounting, the term reserve is most commonly used to describe any part of shareholders' equity, except for basic share capital. In nonprofit accounting, an 'operating reserve' is commonly used to refer to unrestricted cash on hand available to sustain an organization, and nonprofit boards usually specify a target of maintaining several months of operating cash or a percentage of their annual income, called an Operating Reserve Ratio. Sometimes, reserve is used in the sense of the term provision; such a use, however, is inconsistent with the terminology suggested by International Accounting Standards Board.
Cash	In English vernacular cash refers to money in the physical form of currency, such as banknotes and coins. In bookkeeping and finance, cash refers to current assets comprising currency or currency equivalents that can be accessed immediately or near-immediately . Cash is seen either as a reserve for payments, in case of a structural or incidental negative cash flow or as a way to avoid a downturn on financial markets.
Saving	Saving is income not spent, or deferred consumption. Methods of saving include putting money aside in a bank or pension plan. Saving also includes reducing expenditures, such as recurring costs.
Savings bank	A savings bank is a financial institution whose primary purpose is accepting savings deposits and paying interest on those deposits.

8. Money, the Price Level, and Inflation

CHAPTER HIGHLIGHTS & NOTES: KEY TERMS, PEOPLE, PLACES, CONCEPTS

	They originated in Europe during the 18th century with the aim of providing access to savings products to all levels in the population. Often associated with social good these early banks were often designed to encourage low income people to save money and have access to banking services.
Deposit insurance	Explicit deposit insurance is a measure implemented in many countries to protect bank depositors, in full or in part, from losses caused by a bank's inability to pay its debts when due. Deposit insurance systems are one component of a financial system safety net that promotes financial stability.
Federal Deposit Insurance Corporation	The Federal Deposit Insurance Corporation is a United States government corporation operating as an independent agency created by the Banking Act of 1933. As of January 2013, it provides deposit insurance guaranteeing the safety of a depositor's accounts in member banks up to $250,000 for each deposit ownership category in each insured bank. As of September 30, 2012, the Federal Deposit Insurance Corporation insured deposits at 7,181 institutions. The Federal Deposit Insurance Corporation also examines and supervises certain financial institutions for safety and soundness, performs certain consumer-protection functions, and manages banks in receiverships (failed banks).
Loan	An introductory rate is an interest rate charged to a customer during the initial stages of a loan. The rate, which can be as low as 0%, is not permanent and after it expires a normal or higher than normal rate will apply. The purpose of the introductory rate is to market the loan to customers and to seem attractive.
Base period	In economics, a base period or reference period is a point in time used as a reference point for comparison with other periods. It is generally used as a benchmark for measuring financial or economic data. Base periods typically provide a point of reference for economic studies, consumer demand, and unemployment benefit claims.
Reserve banking	Fractional-reserve banking is the practice whereby a bank holds reserves in an amount equal to only a portion of the amount of its customers' deposits to satisfy potential demands for withdrawals. Reserves are held at the bank as currency, or as deposits reflected in the bank's accounts at the central bank. Because bank deposits are usually considered money in their own right, fractional-reserve banking permits the money supply to grow to a multiple (called the money multiplier) of the underlying reserves of base money originally created by the central bank.
Federal Reserve	The Federal Reserve System (also known as the Federal Reserve, and informally as the Fed) is the central banking system of the United States. It was created on December 23, 1913, with the enactment of the Federal Reserve Act, largely in response to a series of financial panics, particularly a severe panic in 1907.

8. Money, the Price Level, and Inflation

CHAPTER HIGHLIGHTS & NOTES: KEY TERMS, PEOPLE, PLACES, CONCEPTS

	Over time, the roles and responsibilities of the Federal Reserve System have expanded, and its structure has evolved. Events such as the Great Depression were major factors leading to changes in the system.
Financial innovation	There are several interpretations of the phrase financial innovation. In general, it refers to the creating and marketing of new types of securities.
Innovation	Innovation is the application of better solutions that meet new requirements, unarticulated needs, or existing market needs. This is accomplished through more effective products, processes, services, technologies, or ideas that are readily available to markets, governments and society. The term innovation can be defined as something original and, as consequence, new that 'breaks into' the market or society.
Lehman Brothers	Lehman Brothers Holdings Inc. (former NYSE ticker symbol LEH) was a global financial services firm. Before declaring bankruptcy in 2008, Lehman was the fourth-largest investment bank in the US (behind Goldman Sachs, Morgan Stanley, and Merrill Lynch), doing business in investment banking, equity and fixed-income sales and trading (especially U.S. Treasury securities), research, investment management, private equity, and private banking.
Bank reserves	Bank reserves or central bank reserves are banks' holdings of deposits in accounts with their central bank, plus currency that is physically held in the bank's vault (vault cash). The central banks of some nations set minimum reserve requirements, which require banks to hold deposits at the central bank equivalent to a specified percentage of their liabilities (such as customer deposits). Even when no reserve requirements are set, banks commonly wish to hold some reserves, called desired reserves, against unexpected events such as unusually large net withdrawals by customers or even bank runs.
Federal Open Market Committee	The Federal Open Market Committee, a committee within the Federal Reserve System (the Fed), is charged under United States law with overseeing the nation's open market operations (i.e., the Fed's buying and selling of United States Treasury securities). It is this Federal Reserve committee which makes key decisions about interest rates and the growth of the United States money supply. It is the principal organ of United States national monetary policy.
Federal Reserve Bank	A Federal Reserve Bank is a regional bank of the Federal Reserve System, the central banking system of the United States. There are twelve in total, one for each of the twelve Federal Reserve Districts that were created by the Federal Reserve Act of 1913. The banks are jointly responsible for implementing the monetary policy set forth by the Federal Open Market Committee, and are divided as follows:

8. Money, the Price Level, and Inflation

CHAPTER HIGHLIGHTS & NOTES: KEY TERMS, PEOPLE, PLACES, CONCEPTS

Federal Reserve System	The Federal Reserve System is the central banking system of the United States. It was created on December 23, 1913, with the enactment of the Federal Reserve Act, largely in response to a series of financial panics, particularly a severe panic in 1907. Over time, the roles and responsibilities of the Federal Reserve System have expanded, and its structure has evolved. Events such as the Great Depression were major factors leading to changes in the system.
Monetary policy	Monetary policy is the process by which the monetary authority of a country controls the supply of money, often targeting a rate of interest for the purpose of promoting economic growth and stability. The official goals usually include relatively stable prices and low unemployment. Monetary economics provides insight into how to craft optimal monetary policy.
Open market	The term open market is used generally to refer to a situation close to free trade and in a more specific technical sense to interbank trade in securities. In principle, a fully open market is a completely free market in which all economic actors can trade without any external constraint.
Arbitrage	In economics and finance, arbitrage --such as a bank or brokerage firm. The term is mainly applied to trading in financial instruments, such as bonds, stocks, derivatives, commodities and currencies.
Balance sheet	In financial accounting, a balance sheet or statement of financial position is a summary of the financial balances of a sole proprietorship, a business partnership, a corporation or other business organization, such as an LLC or an LLP. Assets, liabilities and ownership equity are listed as of a specific date, such as the end of its financial year. A balance sheet is often described as a 'snapshot of a company's financial condition'. Of the three basic financial statements, the balance sheet is the only statement which applies to a single point in time of a business' calendar year.
Monetary base	In economics, the monetary base in a country is defined as the portion of the commercial banks' reserves that are maintained in accounts with their central bank plus the total currency circulating in the public (which includes the currency, also known as vault cash, that is physically held in the banks' vault). The monetary base should not be confused with the money supply which consists of the total currency circulating in the public plus the non-bank deposits with commercial banks.
Mortgage-backed security	A mortgage-backed security is a type of asset-backed security that is secured by a mortgage, or more commonly a collection ('pool') of sometimes hundreds of mortgages. The mortgages are sold to a group of individuals (a government agency or investment bank) that 'securitizes', or packages, the loans together into a security that can be sold to investors. The mortgages of an Mortgage backed security may be residential or commercial, depending on whether it is an Agency Mortgage backed security or a Non-Agency Mortgage backed security; in the United States they may be issued by structures set up by government-sponsored enterprises like Fannie Mae or Freddie Mac, or they can be 'private-label', issued by structures set up by investment banks.

8. Money, the Price Level, and Inflation

CHAPTER HIGHLIGHTS & NOTES: KEY TERMS, PEOPLE, PLACES, CONCEPTS

Open market operation	An open market operation is an activity by a central bank to buy or sell government bonds on the open market. A central bank uses them as the primary means of implementing monetary policy. The usual aim of open market operations is to manipulate the short term interest rate and the supply of base money in an economy, and thus indirectly control the total money supply, in effect expanding money or contracting the money supply.
Asset	An 'asset' in economic theory is an output good which can only be partially consumed or input as a factor of production (like a cement mixer) which can only be partially used up in production. The necessary quality for an asset is that value remains after the period of analysis so it can be used as a store of value. As such, financial instruments like corporate bonds and common stocks are assets because they store value for the next period.
Financial crisis	The term financial crisis is applied broadly to a variety of situations in which some financial assets suddenly lose a large part of their nominal value. In the 19th and early 20th centuries, many financial crises were associated with banking panics, and many recessions coincided with these panics. Other situations that are often called financial crises include stock market crashes and the bursting of other financial bubbles, currency crises, and sovereign defaults.
Recession	In economics, a recession is a business cycle contraction. It is a general slowdown in economic activity. Macroeconomic indicators such as GDP (gross domestic product), investment spending, capacity utilization, household income, business profits, and inflation fall, while bankruptcies and the unemployment rate rise.
Lender of last resort	The term lender of last resort originates from the French expression dernier ressort. While the concept itself had been used previously, the term, 'lender of last resort', was supposedly first used in its current context by Sir Francis Baring in his Observations on the Establishment of the Bank of England which was published in 1797. In 1763 the king was the lender of last resort in Prussia. Different definitions of the lender of last resort exist in the literature.
Excess reserves	In banking, excess reserves are bank reserves in excess of a reserve requirement set by a central bank. They are reserves of cash more than the required amounts. In the United States, bank reserves are held as FRB (Federal Reserve Bank) credit in FRB accounts; they are not separated into separate 'minimum reserves' and 'excess reserves' accounts
Money creation	In economics, money creation is the process by which the money supply of a country or a monetary region is increased. A central bank may introduce new money into the economy (termed 'expansionary monetary policy') by purchasing financial assets or lending money to financial institutions. Commercial bank lending also creates money under the form of demand deposits).
Money multiplier	In monetary economics, a money multiplier is one of various closely related ratios of commercial bank money to central bank money under a fractional-reserve banking system.

8. Money, the Price Level, and Inflation

CHAPTER HIGHLIGHTS & NOTES: KEY TERMS, PEOPLE, PLACES, CONCEPTS

	Most often, it measures the maximum amount of commercial bank money that can be created by a given unit of central bank money. That is, in a fractional-reserve banking system, the total amount of loans that commercial banks are allowed to extend (the commercial bank money that they can legally create) is a multiple of reserves; this multiple is the reciprocal of the reserve ratio, and it is an economic multiplier.
Quantitative easing	Quantitative easing is an unconventional monetary policy used by central banks to stimulate the economy when standard monetary policy has become ineffective. A central bank implements quantitative easing by buying specified amounts of financial assets from commercial banks and other private institutions, thus raising the prices of those financial assets and lowering their yield, while simultaneously increasing the monetary base. This is distinguished from the more usual policy of buying or selling short term government bonds in order to keep interbank interest rates at a specified target value.
Interest rate	An interest rate is the rate at which interest is paid by a borrower for the use of money that they borrow from a lender (creditor). Specifically, the interest rate is a percent of principal (P) paid a certain amount of times (m) per period (usually quoted per annum). For example, a small company borrows capital from a bank to buy new assets for its business, and in return the lender receives interest at a predetermined interest rate for deferring the use of funds and instead lending it to the borrower.
Nominal interest rate	In finance and economics, nominal interest rate or nominal rate of interest refers to two distinct things: the rate of interest before adjustment for inflation ; or, for interest rates 'as stated' without adjustment for the full effect of compounding (also referred to as the nominal annual rate). An interest rate is called nominal if the frequency of compounding (e.g. a month) is not identical to the basic time unit (normally a year).
Nominal money	Nominal money, in economics, is the quantity of money measured in a particular currency and is directly proportional to the price level. This means, among other things, that if the price level rises by 10%, 10% more money than before is necessary in order to maintain stability. For example, a $20 item will cost $22 after the price level increases by 10%.
Price	In ordinary usage, price is the quantity of payment or compensation given by one party to another in return for goods or services. In modern economies, prices are generally expressed in units of some form of currency. (For commodities, they are expressed as currency per unit weight of the commodity, e.g. euros per kilogram).

8. Money, the Price Level, and Inflation

CHAPTER HIGHLIGHTS & NOTES: KEY TERMS, PEOPLE, PLACES, CONCEPTS

Price level	The general price level is a hypothetical measure of overall prices for some set of goods and services, in a given region during a given interval, normalized relative to some base set. Typically, a price level is approximated with a price index.
Real GDP	Real Gross Domestic Product (real GDP) is a macroeconomic measure of the value of economic output adjusted for price changes. This adjustment transforms the money-value measure, nominal GDP, into an index for quantity of total output. GDP is the sum of consumer Spending, Investment made by industry, Excess of Exports over Imports and Government Spending.
Demand	In economics, demand for a good or service is an entire listing of the quantity of the good or service that a market would choose to buy, for every possible market price of the good or service. (Note: This distinguishes 'demand' from 'quantity demanded', where demand is a listing or graphing of quantity demanded at each possible price. In contrast to demand, quantity demanded is the exact quantity demanded at a certain price.
Demand for money	The Baumol-Tobin model is an economic model of the transactions demand for money as developed independently by William Baumol and James Tobin (1956). The theory relies on the tradeoff between the liquidity provided by holding money (the ability to carry out transactions) and the interest forgone by holding one's assets in the form of non-interest bearing money. The key variables of the demand for money are then the nominal interest rate, the level of real income which corresponds to the amount of desired transactions, and the fixed transaction costs of transferring one's wealth between liquid money and interest-bearing assets.
Supply	In economics, supply refers to the amount of a product that producers and firms are willing to sell at a given price all other factors being held constant. Usually, supply is plotted as a supply curve showing the relationship of price to the amount of product businesses are willing to sell.
Money supply	In economics, the money supply or money stock, is the total amount of monetary assets available in an economy at a specific time. There are several ways to define 'money,' but standard measures usually include currency in circulation and demand deposits (depositors' easily accessed assets on the books of financial institutions). It is easy to confuse the amount of spending money in the economy with the amount of money in the economy.
Short run	In microeconomics, the long run is the conceptual time period in which there are no fixed factors of production, so that there are no constraints preventing changing the output level by changing the capital stock or by entering or leaving an industry. The long run contrasts with the short run, in which some factors are variable and others are fixed, constraining entry or exit from an industry. In macroeconomics, the long run is the period when the general price level, contractual wage rates, and expectations adjust fully to the state of the economy, in contrast to the short run when these variables may not fully adjust.

8. Money, the Price Level, and Inflation

CHAPTER HIGHLIGHTS & NOTES: KEY TERMS, PEOPLE, PLACES, CONCEPTS

Quantity theory	In monetary economics, the quantity theory of money states that money supply has a direct, proportional relationship with the price level. While mainstream economists agree that the quantity theory holds true in the long run, there is still disagreement about its applicability in the short run. Critics of the theory argue that money velocity is not stable and, in the short-run, prices are sticky, so the direct relationship between money supply and price level does not hold.
Exchange	An exchange, or bourse, is a highly organized market where tradable securities, commodities, foreign exchange, futures, and options contracts are sold and bought.
Inflation	In economics, inflation is a sustained increase in the general price level of goods and services in an economy over a period of time. When the general price level rises, each unit of currency buys fewer goods and services. Consequently, inflation reflects a reduction in the purchasing power per unit of money - a loss of real value in the medium of exchange and unit of account within the economy.
Interest	Interest is a fee paid by a borrower of assets to the owner as a form of compensation for the use of the assets. It is most commonly the price paid for the use of borrowed money, or money earned by deposited funds. When money is borrowed, interest is typically paid to the lender as a percentage of the principal, the amount owed to the lender.
Rate	In mathematics, a rate is a ratio between two measurements with different units. If the unit or quantity in respect of which something is changing is not specified, usually the rate is per unit time. However, a rate of change can be specified per unit time, or per unit of length or mass or another quantity.
Reserve ratio	The reserve requirement (or cash reserve ratio) is a central bank regulation employed by most, but not all, of the world's central banks, that sets the minimum fraction of customer deposits and notes that each commercial bank must hold as reserves . These required reserves are normally in the form of cash stored physically in a bank vault (vault cash) or deposits made with a central bank. The required reserve ratio is sometimes used as a tool in monetary policy, influencing the country's borrowing and interest rates by changing the amount of funds available for banks to make loans with.

8. Money, the Price Level, and Inflation

CHAPTER QUIZ: KEY TERMS, PEOPLE, PLACES, CONCEPTS

1. A _____ is a remarkable concurrence of events or circumstances which have no apparent causal connection with each other. The perception of remarkable _____s may lead to supernatural, occult, or paranormal claims. Or it may lead to belief in fatalism, which is a doctrine that events will happen in the exact manner of a predetermined plan.

    a. Gresham's Law
    b. Bad bank
    c. Coincidence
    d. Bank code

2. _____ is a system of exchange where goods or services are directly exchanged for other goods or services without using a medium of exchange, such as money. It is distinguishable from gift economies in many ways; one of them is that the reciprocal exchange is immediate and not delayed in time. It is usually bilateral, but may be multilateral (i.e., mediated through _____ organizations) and, in most developed countries, usually only exists parallel to monetary systems to a very limited extent.

    a. Gresham's Law
    b. Federal Reserve
    c. Nash equilibrium
    d. Barter

3. The general _____ is a hypothetical measure of overall prices for some set of goods and services, in a given region during a given interval, normalized relative to some base set. Typically, a _____ is approximated with a price index.

    a. Price level
    b. Broad money
    c. Cambridge equation
    d. Cash-in-advance constraint

4. In the United States, the _____ is the interest rate at which depository institutions actively trade balances held at the Federal Reserve, called federal funds, with each other, usually overnight, on an uncollateralized basis. Institutions with surplus balances in their accounts lend those balances to institutions in need of larger balances. The _____ is an important benchmark in financial markets.

    a. Beige Book
    b. Federal funds rate
    c. CPFF
    d. Credit channel

5. . In English vernacular _____ refers to money in the physical form of currency, such as banknotes and coins.

    In bookkeeping and finance, _____ refers to current assets comprising currency or currency equivalents that can be accessed immediately or near-immediately . _____ is seen either as a reserve for payments, in case of a structural or incidental negative _____ flow or as a way to avoid a downturn on financial markets.

8. Money, the Price Level, and Inflation

CHAPTER QUIZ: KEY TERMS, PEOPLE, PLACES, CONCEPTS

a. Bill of credit
b. Cash
c. medium of exchange
d. Money burning

ANSWER KEY
8. Money, the Price Level, and Inflation

1. c
2. d
3. a
4. b
5. b

You can take the complete Online Interactive Chapter Practice Test

for 8. Money, the Price Level, and Inflation
on all key terms, persons, places, and concepts.

No Additional Costs

http://www.Cram101.com

Register, send an email request to Travis.Reese@Cram101.com to get your user Id and password.

Include your customer order number, and ISBN number from your studyguide Retailer.

9. The Exchange Rate and the Balance of Payments

CHAPTER OUTLINE: KEY TERMS, PEOPLE, PLACES, CONCEPTS

	Bank
	Depreciation
	Dollar
	Euro
	Exchange
	Exchange rate
	Index
	Management
	Market
	Price
	Rate
	Demand
	Demand for money
	Law of demand
	Supply
	Money
	Money supply
	Law of supply
	Supply curve
	Export
	Interest rate

9. The Exchange Rate and the Balance of Payments
CHAPTER OUTLINE: KEY TERMS, PEOPLE, PLACES, CONCEPTS

	Market equilibrium
	Interest
	Bank of Japan
	Arbitrage
	Interest rate parity
	Law of one price
	Purchasing power
	Purchasing power parity
	Big Mac Index
	Speculation
	Price level
	Fixed exchange rate
	Crawling peg
	Balance
	Capital
	Current account
	Payment
	Reserve
	Trade
	Loanable funds
	Creditor

9. The Exchange Rate and the Balance of Payments

CHAPTER OUTLINE: KEY TERMS, PEOPLE, PLACES, CONCEPTS

	Debtor
	Human capital
	Consumption
	Good
	Income
	National income
	National Income and Product Accounts
	Private sector
	Product
	Balance of payments
	Open market
	Great Depression
	Macroeconomics

9. The Exchange Rate and the Balance of Payments

CHAPTER HIGHLIGHTS & NOTES: KEY TERMS, PEOPLE, PLACES, CONCEPTS

Bank	A bank is a financial institution and a financial intermediary that accepts deposits and channels those deposits into lending activities, either directly by loaning or indirectly through capital markets. A bank links together customers that have capital deficits and customers with capital surpluses. Due to their influential status within the financial system and upon national economies, banks are highly regulated in most countries.
Depreciation	In accountancy, depreciation refers to two aspects of the same concept:•the decrease in value of assets (fair value depreciation), and•the allocation of the cost of assets to periods in which the assets are used (depreciation with the matching principle). The former affects the balance sheet of a business or entity, and the latter affects the net income that they report. Generally the cost is allocated, as depreciation expense, among the periods in which the asset is expected to be used. This expense is recognized by businesses for financial reporting and tax purposes.
Dollar	Dollar is the name of several currencies, including those of Australia, Belize, Brunei, Canada, Hong Kong, Namibia, New Zealand, Singapore, Taiwan, the United States, and previously Zimbabwe. The U.S. dollar is the official currency of East Timor, Ecuador, El Salvador, Federated States of Micronesia, Marshall Islands, Palau, the Caribbean Netherlands, and for banknotes, Panama. Generally, one dollar is divided into one hundred cents.
Euro	The euro is the currency used by the Institutions of the European Union and is the official currency of the eurozone, which consists of 18 of the 28 member states of the European Union: Austria, Belgium, Cyprus, Estonia, Finland, France, Germany, Greece, Ireland, Italy, Latvia, Luxembourg, Malta, the Netherlands, Portugal, Slovakia, Slovenia, and Spain. The currency is also used in a further five European countries and consequently used daily by some 334 million Europeans as of 2013. Additionally, 210 million people worldwide as of 2013-- including 182 million people in Africa--use currencies pegged to the euro. The euro is the second largest reserve currency as well as the second most traded currency in the world after the United States dollar.
Exchange	An exchange, or bourse, is a highly organized market where tradable securities, commodities, foreign exchange, futures, and options contracts are sold and bought.
Exchange rate	In finance, an exchange rate between two currencies is the rate at which one currency will be exchanged for another. It is also regarded as the value of one country's currency in terms of another currency. For example, an interbank exchange rate of 91 Japanese yen (JPY, ¥) to the United States dollar (US$) means that ¥91 will be exchanged for each US$1 or that US$1 will be exchanged for each ¥91.

9. The Exchange Rate and the Balance of Payments

CHAPTER HIGHLIGHTS & NOTES: KEY TERMS, PEOPLE, PLACES, CONCEPTS

	Exchange rates are determined in the foreign exchange market, which is open to a wide range of different types of buyers and sellers where currency trading is continuous: 24 hours a day except weekends, i.e. trading from 20:15 GMT on Sunday until 22:00 GMT Friday.
Index	In economics and finance, an index is a statistical measure of changes in a representative group of individual data points. These data may be derived from any number of sources, including company performance, prices, productivity, and employment. Economic indices (index, plural) track economic health from different perspectives.
Management	Management in businesses and other organizations, including not-for-profit organizations and government bodies, refers to the individuals who set the strategy of the organization and coordinate the efforts of employees to accomplish objectives by using available human, financial and other resources efficiently and effectively. Resourcing encompasses the deployment and manipulation of human resources, financial resources, technological resources, natural resources and other resources. Management is also an academic discipline, a social science whose objective is to study social organization and organizational leadership.
Market	A financial market is a market in which people and entities can trade financial securities, commodities, and other fungible items of value at low transaction costs and at prices that reflect supply and demand. Securities include stocks and bonds, and commodities include precious metals or agricultural goods. There are both general markets (where many commodities are traded) and specialized markets (where only one commodity is traded).
Price	In ordinary usage, price is the quantity of payment or compensation given by one party to another in return for goods or services. In modern economies, prices are generally expressed in units of some form of currency. (For commodities, they are expressed as currency per unit weight of the commodity, e.g. euros per kilogram).
Rate	In mathematics, a rate is a ratio between two measurements with different units. If the unit or quantity in respect of which something is changing is not specified, usually the rate is per unit time. However, a rate of change can be specified per unit time, or per unit of length or mass or another quantity.
Demand	In economics, demand for a good or service is an entire listing of the quantity of the good or service that a market would choose to buy, for every possible market price of the good or service.

9. The Exchange Rate and the Balance of Payments

CHAPTER HIGHLIGHTS & NOTES: KEY TERMS, PEOPLE, PLACES, CONCEPTS

	(Note: This distinguishes 'demand' from 'quantity demanded', where demand is a listing or graphing of quantity demanded at each possible price. In contrast to demand, quantity demanded is the exact quantity demanded at a certain price.
Demand for money	The Baumol-Tobin model is an economic model of the transactions demand for money as developed independently by William Baumol and James Tobin (1956). The theory relies on the tradeoff between the liquidity provided by holding money (the ability to carry out transactions) and the interest forgone by holding one's assets in the form of non-interest bearing money. The key variables of the demand for money are then the nominal interest rate, the level of real income which corresponds to the amount of desired transactions, and the fixed transaction costs of transferring one's wealth between liquid money and interest-bearing assets.
Law of demand	In economics, the law states that, all else being equal, as the price of a product increases, quantity demanded falls; likewise, as the price of a product decreases, quantity demanded increases. In other words, the law of demand states that the quantity demanded and the price of a commodity are inversely related, other things remaining constant. If the income of the consumer, prices of the related goods, and preferences of the consumer remain unchanged, then the change in quantity of good demanded by the consumer will be negatively correlated to the change in the price of the good.
Supply	In economics, supply refers to the amount of a product that producers and firms are willing to sell at a given price all other factors being held constant. Usually, supply is plotted as a supply curve showing the relationship of price to the amount of product businesses are willing to sell.
Money	Monetary disequilibrium theory is basically a product of the Monetarist school mainly represented in the works of Leland Yeager and Austrian macroeconomics. The basic concept of monetary equilibrium (disequilibrium) was, however, defined in terms of an individual's demand for cash balance by Mises (1912) in his Theory of Money and Credit. Monetary Disequilibrium is one of three theories of macroeconomic fluctuations which accord an important role to money, the others being the Austrian theory of the business cycle and one based on rational expectations.
Money supply	In economics, the money supply or money stock, is the total amount of monetary assets available in an economy at a specific time. There are several ways to define 'money,' but standard measures usually include currency in circulation and demand deposits (depositors' easily accessed assets on the books of financial institutions). It is easy to confuse the amount of spending money in the economy with the amount of money in the economy.
Law of supply	The law of supply is a fundamental principle of economic theory which states that, all else equal, an increase in price results in an increase in quantity supplied.

9. The Exchange Rate and the Balance of Payments

CHAPTER HIGHLIGHTS & NOTES: KEY TERMS, PEOPLE, PLACES, CONCEPTS

	In other words, there is a direct relationship between price and quantity: quantities respond in the same direction as price changes. This means that producers are willing to offer more products for sale on the market at higher prices by increasing production as a way of increasing profits.
Supply curve	In microeconomics, supply and demand is an economic model of price determination in a market. It concludes that in a competitive market, the unit price for a particular good will vary until it settles at a point where the quantity demanded by consumers (at current price) will equal the quantity supplied by producers (at current price), resulting in an economic equilibrium for price and quantity. The four basic laws of supply and demand are:•If demand increases (demand curve shifts to the right) and supply remains unchanged, a shortage occurs, leading to a higher equilibrium price.•If demand decreases (demand curve shifts to the left) supply remains unchanged, a surplus occurs, leading to a lower equilibrium price.•If demand remains unchanged and supply increases (supply curve shifts to the right), a surplus occurs, leading to a lower equilibrium price.•If demand remains unchanged and supply decreases (supply curve shifts to the left), a shortage occurs, leading to a higher equilibrium price.
Export	The term export means shipping the goods and services out of the port of a country. The seller of such goods and services is referred to as an 'exporter' who is based in the country of export whereas the overseas based buyer is referred to as an 'importer'. In International Trade, 'exports' refers to selling goods and services produced in the home country to other markets.
Interest rate	An interest rate is the rate at which interest is paid by a borrower for the use of money that they borrow from a lender (creditor). Specifically, the interest rate is a percent of principal (P) paid a certain amount of times (m) per period (usually quoted per annum). For example, a small company borrows capital from a bank to buy new assets for its business, and in return the lender receives interest at a predetermined interest rate for deferring the use of funds and instead lending it to the borrower.
Market equilibrium	In economics, economic equilibrium is a state where economic forces such as supply and demand are balanced and in the absence of external influences the values of economic variables will not change. For example, in the standard text-book model of perfect competition, equilibrium occurs at the point at which quantity demanded and quantity supplied are equal. Market equilibrium in this case refers to a condition where a market price is established through competition such that the amount of goods or services sought by buyers is equal to the amount of goods or services produced by sellers.
Interest	Interest is a fee paid by a borrower of assets to the owner as a form of compensation for the use of the assets. It is most commonly the price paid for the use of borrowed money, or money earned by deposited funds.

9. The Exchange Rate and the Balance of Payments

CHAPTER HIGHLIGHTS & NOTES: KEY TERMS, PEOPLE, PLACES, CONCEPTS

Bank of Japan	The Bank of Japan is the central bank of Japan. The Bank is often called Nichigin for short. It has its headquarters in Chuo, Tokyo.
Arbitrage	In economics and finance, arbitrage --such as a bank or brokerage firm. The term is mainly applied to trading in financial instruments, such as bonds, stocks, derivatives, commodities and currencies.
Interest rate parity	Interest rate parity is a no-arbitrage condition representing an equilibrium state under which investors will be indifferent to interest rates available on bank deposits in two countries. The fact that this condition does not always hold allows for potential opportunities to earn riskless profits from covered interest arbitrage. Two assumptions central to interest rate parity are capital mobility and perfect substitutability of domestic and foreign assets.
Law of one price	The law of one price is an economic concept which posits that 'a good must sell for the same price in all locations'. The law of one price constitutes the basis of the theory of purchasing power parity and is derived from the no arbitrage assumption .
Purchasing power	Purchasing power is the number of goods or services that can be purchased with a unit of currency. For example, if one had taken one unit of currency to a store in the 1950s, it is probable that it would have been possible to buy a greater number of items than would today, indicating that one would have had a greater purchasing power in the 1950s. Currency can be either a commodity money, like gold or silver, or fiat currency, or free-floating market-valued currency like US dollars.
Purchasing power parity	Purchasing power parity is a component of some economic theories and is a technique used to determine the relative value of different currencies. Theories that invoke purchasing power parity assume that in some circumstances (for example, as a long-run tendency) it would cost exactly the same number of, say, US dollars to buy euros and then to use the proceeds to buy a market basket of goods as it would cost to use those dollars directly in purchasing the market basket of goods. The concept of purchasing power parity allows one to estimate what the exchange rate between two currencies would have to be in order for the exchange to be at par with the purchasing power of the two countries' currencies.
Big Mac Index	The Big Mac Index is published by The Economist as an informal way of measuring the purchasing power parity between two currencies and provides a test of the extent to which market exchange rates result in goods costing the same in different countries. It 'seeks to make exchange-rate theory a bit more digestible'. The index takes its name from the Big Mac, a hamburger sold at McDonald's restaurants.

9. The Exchange Rate and the Balance of Payments

CHAPTER HIGHLIGHTS & NOTES: KEY TERMS, PEOPLE, PLACES, CONCEPTS

Speculation	Speculation is the practice of engaging in risky financial transactions in an attempt to profit from short or medium term fluctuations in the market value of a tradable good such as a financial instrument, rather than attempting to profit from the underlying financial attributes embodied in the instrument such as capital gains, interest, or dividends. Many speculators pay little attention to the fundamental value of a security and instead focus purely on price movements. Speculation can in principle involve any tradable good or financial instrument.
Price level	The general price level is a hypothetical measure of overall prices for some set of goods and services, in a given region during a given interval, normalized relative to some base set. Typically, a price level is approximated with a price index.
Fixed exchange rate	A fixed exchange rate, sometimes called a pegged exchange rate, is also referred to as the Tag of particular Rate, which is a type of exchange rate regime where a currency's value is fixed against the value of another single currency, to a basket of other currencies, or to another measure of value, such as gold. A fixed exchange rate is usually used to stabilize the value of a currency against the currency it is pegged to. This makes trade and investments between the two countries easier and more predictable and is especially useful for small economies in which external trade forms a large part of their GDP. It can also be used as a means to control inflation.
Crawling peg	Crawling peg is an exchange rate regime usually seen as a part of fixed exchange rate regimes that allows depreciation or appreciation in an exchange rate gradually.The system is a method to fully utilize the key under the fixed exchange regimes as well as the flexibility under the floating exchange rate regime. The system is shaped to peg at a certain value but at the same time is designed to "glide" to response to external market uncertainties. In dealing to external pressure (such as interest rate differentials or changes in foreign exchange reserves) to appreciate or depreciate the exchange rate, the system can meet frequent but moderate exchange rate changes to ensure that the economic dislocation is kept minimal.
Balance	In banking and accountancy, the outstanding balance is the amount of money owed that remains in a deposit account (or a loan account) at a given date, after all past remittances, payments and withdrawal have been accounted for. It can be positive (then, in the balance sheet of a firm, it is an asset) or negative (a liability).
Capital	In economics, capital goods, real capital, or capital assets are already-produced durable goods or any non-financial asset that is used in production of goods or services. Capital goods are not significantly consumed in the production process though they may depreciate.

9. The Exchange Rate and the Balance of Payments

CHAPTER HIGHLIGHTS & NOTES: KEY TERMS, PEOPLE, PLACES, CONCEPTS

Current account	In economics, a country's current account is one of the two components of its balance of payments, the other being the capital account. The current account consists of the balance of trade, net factor income (earnings on foreign investments minus payments made to foreign investors) and cash transfers. The current account balance is one of two major measures of a country's foreign trade (the other being the net capital outflow).
Payment	A payment is the transfer of an item of value from one party to another in exchange for the provision of goods, services or both, or to fulfill a legal obligation. The simplest and oldest form of payment is barter, the exchange of one good or service for another. In the modern world, common means of payment by an individual include money, cheque, debit, credit, or bank transfer, and in trade such payments are frequently preceded by an invoice or result in a receipt.
Reserve	In financial accounting, the term reserve is most commonly used to describe any part of shareholders' equity, except for basic share capital. In nonprofit accounting, an 'operating reserve' is commonly used to refer to unrestricted cash on hand available to sustain an organization, and nonprofit boards usually specify a target of maintaining several months of operating cash or a percentage of their annual income, called an Operating Reserve Ratio. Sometimes, reserve is used in the sense of the term provision; such a use, however, is inconsistent with the terminology suggested by International Accounting Standards Board.
Trade	In finance, a trade is an exchange of a security for 'cash', typically a short-dated promise to pay in the currency of the country where the 'exchange' is located.
Loanable funds	In economics, the loanable funds market is a hypothetical market that brings savers and borrowers together, also bringing together the money available in commercial banks and lending institutions available for firms and households to finance expenditures, either investments or consumption. Savers supply the loanable funds; for instance, buying bonds will transfer their money to the institution issuing the bond, which can be a firm or government. In return, borrowers demand loanable funds; when an institution sells a bond, it is demanding loanable funds.
Creditor	A creditor is a party that has a claim on the services of a second party. It is a person or institution to whom money is owed. The first party, in general, has provided some property or service to the second party under the assumption (usually enforced by contract) that the second party will return an equivalent property and service.
Debtor	A debtor is an entity that owes a debt to another entity. The entity may be an individual, a firm, a government, a company or other legal person.

9. The Exchange Rate and the Balance of Payments

CHAPTER HIGHLIGHTS & NOTES: KEY TERMS, PEOPLE, PLACES, CONCEPTS

Human capital	Human capital is the stock of competencies, knowledge, habits, social and personality attributes, including creativity, cognitive abilities, embodied in the ability to perform labor so as to produce economic value. It is an aggregate economic view of the human being acting within economies, which is an attempt to capture the social, biological, cultural and psychological complexity as they interact in explicit and/or economic transactions. Many theories explicitly connect investment in human capital development to education, and the role of human capital in economic development, productivity growth, and innovation has frequently been cited as a justification for government subsidies for education and job skills training.
Consumption	Consumption is a major concept in economics and is also studied by many other social sciences. Economists are particularly interested in the relationship between consumption and income, and therefore in economics the consumption function plays a major role. Different schools of economists define production and consumption differently.
Good	In economics, a good is a material that satisfies human wants and provides utility, for example, to a consumer making a purchase. A common distinction is made between 'goods' that are tangible property (also called goods) and services, which are non-physical. Commodities may be used as a synonym for economic goods but often refer to marketable raw materials and primary products.
Income	Income is the consumption and savings opportunity gained by an entity within a specified timeframe, which is generally expressed in monetary terms. However, for households and individuals, 'income is the sum of all the wages, salaries, profits, interests payments, rents and other forms of earnings received... in a given period of time.' In the field of public economics, the term may refer to the accumulation of both monetary and non-monetary consumption ability, with the former (monetary) being used as a proxy for total income.
National income	A variety of measures of national income and output are used in economics to estimate total economic activity in a country or region, including gross domestic product, gross national product (GNP), net national income and adjusted national income. All are specially concerned with counting the total amount of goods and services produced within some 'boundary'. The boundary is usually defined by geography or citizenship, and may also restrict the goods and services that are counted.
National Income and Product Accounts	The national income and product accounts are part of the national accounts of the United States. They are produced by the Bureau of Economic Analysis of the Department of Commerce. They are one of the main sources of data on general economic activity in the United States.
Private sector	The private sector is that part of the economy, sometimes referred to as the citizen sector, which is run by private individuals or groups, usually as a means of enterprise for profit, and is not controlled by the state .

9. The Exchange Rate and the Balance of Payments

CHAPTER HIGHLIGHTS & NOTES: KEY TERMS, PEOPLE, PLACES, CONCEPTS

Product	In marketing, a product is anything that can be offered to a market that might satisfy a want or need. In retailing, products are called merchandise. In manufacturing, products are bought as raw materials and sold as finished goods.
Balance of payments	Balance of Payment of a country is defined as, 'Systematic record of all economic transactions between the residents of a foreign country' Thus balance of payments includes all visible and non-visible transactions of a country during a given period, usually a year. It represents a summation of country's current demand and supply of the claims on foreign currencies and of foreign claims on its currency. Balance of payments accounts are an accounting record of all monetary transactions between a country and the rest of the world.
Open market	The term open market is used generally to refer to a situation close to free trade and in a more specific technical sense to interbank trade in securities. In principle, a fully open market is a completely free market in which all economic actors can trade without any external constraint.
Great Depression	The Great Depression was a severe worldwide economic depression in the decade preceding World War II. The timing of the Great Depression varied across nations, but in most countries it started in 1930 and lasted until the late 1930s or middle 1940s. It was the longest, deepest, and most widespread depression of the 20th century. In the 21st century, the Great Depression is commonly used as an example of how far the world's economy can decline.
Macroeconomics	Macroeconomics is a branch of economics dealing with the performance, structure, behavior, and decision-making of an economy as a whole, rather than individual markets. This includes national, regional, and global economies. With microeconomics, macroeconomics is one of the two most general fields in economics.

9. The Exchange Rate and the Balance of Payments

CHAPTER QUIZ: KEY TERMS, PEOPLE, PLACES, CONCEPTS

1. In economics, _____ for a good or service is an entire listing of the quantity of the good or service that a market would choose to buy, for every possible market price of the good or service. (Note: This distinguishes '_____' from 'quantity demanded', where _____ is a listing or graphing of quantity demanded at each possible price. In contrast to _____, quantity demanded is the exact quantity demanded at a certain price.

   a. Bad bank
   b. Bank failure
   c. Demand
   d. Communist Bund

2. The _____ is a fundamental principle of economic theory which states that, all else equal, an increase in price results in an increase in quantity supplied. In other words, there is a direct relationship between price and quantity: quantities respond in the same direction as price changes. This means that producers are willing to offer more products for sale on the market at higher prices by increasing production as a way of increasing profits.

   a. Law of supply
   b. Law of reflux
   c. Law of rent
   d. The New York Pizza Connection

3. A _____ is the transfer of an item of value from one party to another in exchange for the provision of goods, services or both, or to fulfill a legal obligation.

   The simplest and oldest form of _____ is barter, the exchange of one good or service for another. In the modern world, common means of _____ by an individual include money, cheque, debit, credit, or bank transfer, and in trade such _____s are frequently preceded by an invoice or result in a receipt.

   a. Base period
   b. Benefit incidence
   c. Payment
   d. Bond

4. An _____, or bourse, is a highly organized market where tradable securities, commodities, foreign _____, futures, and options contracts are sold and bought.

   a. Bagholder
   b. Barbell strategy
   c. BATS Chi-X Europe
   d. Exchange

5. . In economics, the _____ or money stock, is the total amount of monetary assets available in an economy at a specific time. There are several ways to define 'money,' but standard measures usually include currency in circulation and demand deposits (depositors' easily accessed assets on the books of financial institutions).

9. The Exchange Rate and the Balance of Payments

CHAPTER QUIZ: KEY TERMS, PEOPLE, PLACES, CONCEPTS

It is easy to confuse the amount of spending money in the economy with the amount of money in the economy.

a. Base effect
b. Built-in inflation
c. Chronic inflation
d. Money supply

ANSWER KEY
9. The Exchange Rate and the Balance of Payments

1. c
2. a
3. c
4. d
5. d

You can take the complete Online Interactive Chapter Practice Test

for 9. The Exchange Rate and the Balance of Payments
on all key terms, persons, places, and concepts.

No Additional Costs

http://www.Cram101.com

Register, send an email request to Travis.Reese@Cram101.com to get your user Id and password.

Include your customer order number, and ISBN number from your studyguide Retailer.

10. Aggregate Supply and Aggregate Demand

CHAPTER OUTLINE: KEY TERMS, PEOPLE, PLACES, CONCEPTS

	Full employment
	Real GDP
	Price
	Price level
	Aggregate supply
	Supply
	Human capital
	Quantitative easing
	Capital
	Money
	Multiplier
	Wage
	Aggregate demand
	Wealth effect
	Demand curve
	Relative price
	Demand
	Fiscal policy
	Monetary policy
	Recessionary gap
	World economy

10. Aggregate Supply and Aggregate Demand
CHAPTER OUTLINE: KEY TERMS, PEOPLE, PLACES, CONCEPTS

- Dollar
- Economy
- Exchange
- Exchange rate
- Rate
- Macroeconomics
- Economic growth
- Inflation
- Business cycle
- Inflationary gap
- Output gap
- Stagflation
- New classical macroeconomics
- New Keynesian
- Monetarist
- Congressional Budget Office

10. Aggregate Supply and Aggregate Demand

CHAPTER HIGHLIGHTS & NOTES: KEY TERMS, PEOPLE, PLACES, CONCEPTS

Full employment	Full employment, in macroeconomics, is the level of employment rates where there is no cyclical or deficient-demand unemployment. It is defined by the majority of mainstream economists as being an acceptable level of unemployment somewhere above 0%. The discrepancy from 0% arises due to non-cyclical types of unemployment.
Real GDP	Real Gross Domestic Product (real GDP) is a macroeconomic measure of the value of economic output adjusted for price changes . This adjustment transforms the money-value measure, nominal GDP, into an index for quantity of total output. GDP is the sum of consumer Spending, Investment made by industry, Excess of Exports over Imports and Government Spending.
Price	In ordinary usage, price is the quantity of payment or compensation given by one party to another in return for goods or services. In modern economies, prices are generally expressed in units of some form of currency. (For commodities, they are expressed as currency per unit weight of the commodity, e.g. euros per kilogram).
Price level	The general price level is a hypothetical measure of overall prices for some set of goods and services, in a given region during a given interval, normalized relative to some base set. Typically, a price level is approximated with a price index.
Aggregate supply	In economics, aggregate supply is the total supply of goods and services that firms in a national economy plan on selling during a specific time period. It is the total amount of goods and services that firms are willing to sell at a given price level in an economy.
Supply	In economics, supply refers to the amount of a product that producers and firms are willing to sell at a given price all other factors being held constant. Usually, supply is plotted as a supply curve showing the relationship of price to the amount of product businesses are willing to sell.
Human capital	Human capital is the stock of competencies, knowledge, habits, social and personality attributes, including creativity, cognitive abilities, embodied in the ability to perform labor so as to produce economic value. It is an aggregate economic view of the human being acting within economies, which is an attempt to capture the social, biological, cultural and psychological complexity as they interact in explicit and/or economic transactions. Many theories explicitly connect investment in human capital development to education, and the role of human capital in economic development, productivity growth, and innovation has frequently been cited as a justification for government subsidies for education and job skills training.
Quantitative easing	Quantitative easing is an unconventional monetary policy used by central banks to stimulate the economy when standard monetary policy has become ineffective.

10. Aggregate Supply and Aggregate Demand

CHAPTER HIGHLIGHTS & NOTES: KEY TERMS, PEOPLE, PLACES, CONCEPTS

	A central bank implements quantitative easing by buying specified amounts of financial assets from commercial banks and other private institutions, thus raising the prices of those financial assets and lowering their yield, while simultaneously increasing the monetary base. This is distinguished from the more usual policy of buying or selling short term government bonds in order to keep interbank interest rates at a specified target value.
Capital	In economics, capital goods, real capital, or capital assets are already-produced durable goods or any non-financial asset that is used in production of goods or services.
	Capital goods are not significantly consumed in the production process though they may depreciate. How a capital good or is maintained or returned to its pre-production state varies with the type of capital involved.
Money	Monetary disequilibrium theory is basically a product of the Monetarist school mainly represented in the works of Leland Yeager and Austrian macroeconomics. The basic concept of monetary equilibrium (disequilibrium) was, however, defined in terms of an individual's demand for cash balance by Mises (1912) in his Theory of Money and Credit.
	Monetary Disequilibrium is one of three theories of macroeconomic fluctuations which accord an important role to money, the others being the Austrian theory of the business cycle and one based on rational expectations.
Multiplier	In economics, a multiplier is a factor of proportionality that measures how much an endogenous variable changes in response to a change in some exogenous variable.
	For example, suppose variable x changes by 1 unit, which causes another variable y to change by M units. Then the multiplier is M.
Wage	A wage is monetary compensation paid by an employer to an employee in exchange for work done. Payment may be calculated as a fixed amount for each task completed (a task wage or piece rate), or at an hourly or daily rate, or based on an easily measured quantity of work done.
	Payment by wage contrasts with salaried work, in which the employer pays an arranged amount at steady intervals (such as a week or month) regardless of hours worked, with commission which conditions pay on individual performance, and with compensation based on the performance of the company as a whole.
Aggregate demand	In economics, aggregate behavior refers to relationships between economic aggregates such as national income, government expenditure and aggregate demand. For example, the consumption function is a relationship between aggregate demand for consumption and aggregate disposable income.

10. Aggregate Supply and Aggregate Demand

CHAPTER HIGHLIGHTS & NOTES: KEY TERMS, PEOPLE, PLACES, CONCEPTS

Wealth effect	The wealth effect is an economic term, referring to an increase in spending that accompanies an increase (decrease) in perceived wealth.
Demand curve	In economics, the demand curve is the graph depicting the relationship between the price of a certain commodity and the amount of it that consumers are willing and able to purchase at that given price. It is a graphic representation of a demand schedule. The demand curve for all consumers together follows from the demand curve of every individual consumer: the individual demands at each price are added together.
Relative price	A relative price is the price of a commodity such as a good or service in terms of another; i.e., the ratio of two prices. A relative price may be expressed in terms of a ratio between any two prices or the ratio between the price of one particular good and a weighted average of all other goods available in the market. A relative price is an opportunity cost.
Demand	In economics, demand for a good or service is an entire listing of the quantity of the good or service that a market would choose to buy, for every possible market price of the good or service. (Note: This distinguishes 'demand' from 'quantity demanded', where demand is a listing or graphing of quantity demanded at each possible price. In contrast to demand, quantity demanded is the exact quantity demanded at a certain price.
Fiscal policy	In economics and political science, fiscal policy is the use of government revenue collection and expenditure (spending) to influence the economy. The two main instruments of fiscal policy are changes in the level and composition of taxation and government spending in various sectors. These changes can affect the following macroeconomic variables in an economy:•Aggregate demand and the level of economic activity;•The distribution of income;•The pattern of resource allocation within the government sector and relative to the private sector. Fiscal policy refers to the use of the government budget to influence economic activity.
Monetary policy	Monetary policy is the process by which the monetary authority of a country controls the supply of money, often targeting a rate of interest for the purpose of promoting economic growth and stability. The official goals usually include relatively stable prices and low unemployment. Monetary economics provides insight into how to craft optimal monetary policy.
Recessionary gap	The GDP gap or the output gap is the difference between actual GDP or actual output and potential GDP. The calculation for the output gap is Y-Y* where Y is actual output and Y* is potential output. If this calculation yields a positive number it is called an inflationary gap and indicates the growth of aggregate demand is outpacing the growth of aggregate supply--possibly creating inflation; if the calculation yields a negative number it is called a recessionary gap--possibly signifying deflation. The percentage GDP gap is the actual GDP minus the potential GDP divided by the potential GDP.

10. Aggregate Supply and Aggregate Demand

CHAPTER HIGHLIGHTS & NOTES: KEY TERMS, PEOPLE, PLACES, CONCEPTS

	$(GDP_{actual} - GDP_{potential}) / GDP_{potential}$ {displaystyle {(GDP_{actual}-GDP_{potential})} over {GDP_{potential}}}.
World economy	The world economy, or global economy, generally refers to the economy, which is based on economies of all of the world's countries' national economies. Also global economy can be seen as the economy of global society and national economies - as economies of local societies, making the global one. It can be evaluated in various kind of ways.
Dollar	Dollar is the name of several currencies, including those of Australia, Belize, Brunei, Canada, Hong Kong, Namibia, New Zealand, Singapore, Taiwan, the United States, and previously Zimbabwe. The U.S. dollar is the official currency of East Timor, Ecuador, El Salvador, Federated States of Micronesia, Marshall Islands, Palau, the Caribbean Netherlands, and for banknotes, Panama. Generally, one dollar is divided into one hundred cents.
Economy	An economy or economic system consists of the production, distribution or trade, and consumption of limited goods and services by different agents in a given geographical location. The economic agents can be individuals, businesses, organizations, or governments. Transactions occur when two parties agree to the value or price of the transacted good or service, commonly expressed in a certain currency.
Exchange	An exchange, or bourse, is a highly organized market where tradable securities, commodities, foreign exchange, futures, and options contracts are sold and bought.
Exchange rate	In finance, an exchange rate between two currencies is the rate at which one currency will be exchanged for another. It is also regarded as the value of one country's currency in terms of another currency. For example, an interbank exchange rate of 91 Japanese yen (JPY, ¥) to the United States dollar (US$) means that ¥91 will be exchanged for each US$1 or that US$1 will be exchanged for each ¥91. Exchange rates are determined in the foreign exchange market, which is open to a wide range of different types of buyers and sellers where currency trading is continuous: 24 hours a day except weekends, i.e. trading from 20:15 GMT on Sunday until 22:00 GMT Friday.
Rate	In mathematics, a rate is a ratio between two measurements with different units. If the unit or quantity in respect of which something is changing is not specified, usually the rate is per unit time. However, a rate of change can be specified per unit time, or per unit of length or mass or another quantity.
Macroeconomics	Macroeconomics is a branch of economics dealing with the performance, structure, behavior, and decision-making of an economy as a whole, rather than individual markets. This includes national, regional, and global economies.

10. Aggregate Supply and Aggregate Demand

CHAPTER HIGHLIGHTS & NOTES: KEY TERMS, PEOPLE, PLACES, CONCEPTS

Economic growth	Economic growth is the increase in the market value of the goods and services produced by an economy over time. It is conventionally measured as the percent rate of increase in real gross domestic product, or real GDP. Of more importance is the growth of the ratio of GDP to population (GDP per capita), which is also called per capita income. An increase in per capita income is referred to as intensive growth.
Inflation	In economics, inflation is a sustained increase in the general price level of goods and services in an economy over a period of time. When the general price level rises, each unit of currency buys fewer goods and services. Consequently, inflation reflects a reduction in the purchasing power per unit of money - a loss of real value in the medium of exchange and unit of account within the economy.
Business cycle	The term business cycle refers to economy-wide fluctuations in production, trade and economic activity in general over several months or years in an economy organized on free-enterprise principles. The business cycle is the upward and downward movements of levels of GDP (gross domestic product) and refers to the period of expansions and contractions in the level of economic activities (business fluctuations) around its long-term growth trend. These fluctuations occur around a long-term growth trend, and typically involve shifts over time between periods of relatively rapid economic growth (an expansion or boom), and periods of relative stagnation or decline (a contraction or recession).
Inflationary gap	An inflationary gap, in economics, is the amount by which the actual gross domestic product exceeds potential full-employment GDP. It is one type of output gap, the other being a recessionary gap.
Output gap	The GDP gap or the output gap is the difference between actual GDP or actual output and potential GDP. The calculation for the output gap is Y-Y* where Y is actual output and Y* is potential output. If this calculation yields a positive number it is called an inflationary gap and indicates the growth of aggregate demand is outpacing the growth of aggregate supply--possibly creating inflation; if the calculation yields a negative number it is called a recessionary gap--possibly signifying deflation. The percentage GDP gap is the actual GDP minus the potential GDP divided by the potential GDP. $$\frac{(GDP_{actual} - GDP_{potential})}{GDP_{potential}}$$

10. Aggregate Supply and Aggregate Demand

CHAPTER HIGHLIGHTS & NOTES: KEY TERMS, PEOPLE, PLACES, CONCEPTS

Stagflation	Stagflation, a portmanteau of stagnation and inflation, is a term used in economics to describe a situation where the inflation rate is high, the economic growth rate slows down, and unemployment remains steadily high. It raises a dilemma for economic policy since actions designed to lower inflation may exacerbate unemployment, and vice versa. The term is generally attributed to a British politician who became chancellor of the exchequer in 1970, Iain Macleod, who coined the phrase in his speech to Parliament in 1965. In the version of Keynesian macroeconomic theory which was dominant between the end of WWII and the late-1970s, inflation and recession were regarded as mutually exclusive, the relationship between the two being described by the Phillips curve.
New classical macroeconomics	New classical macroeconomics, sometimes simply called new classical economics, is a school of thought in macroeconomics that builds its analysis entirely on a neoclassical framework. Specifically, it emphasizes the importance of rigorous foundations based on microeconomics, especially rational expectations. New classical macroeconomics strives to provide neoclassical microeconomic foundations for macroeconomic analysis.
New Keynesian	New Keynesian economics is a school of contemporary macroeconomics that strives to provide microeconomic foundations for Keynesian economics. It developed partly as a response to criticisms of Keynesian macroeconomics by adherents of New Classical macroeconomics. Two main assumptions define the New Keynesian approach to macroeconomics.
Monetarist	A monetarist emphasizes the role of governments in controlling the amount of money in circulation. Monetarist theory asserts that variations in the money supply have major influences on national output in the short run and on price levels over longer periods. Monetarists assert that the objectives of monetary policy are best met by targeting the growth rate of the money supply rather than by engaging in discretionary monetary policy.
Congressional Budget Office	The Congressional Budget Office is a federal agency within the legislative branch of the United States government that provides economic data to Congress. The Congressional Budget Office was created as a nonpartisan agency by the Congressional Budget and Impoundment Control Act of 1974.

10. Aggregate Supply and Aggregate Demand

CHAPTER QUIZ: KEY TERMS, PEOPLE, PLACES, CONCEPTS

1. _____ is the name of several currencies, including those of Australia, Belize, Brunei, Canada, Hong Kong, Namibia, New Zealand, Singapore, Taiwan, the United States, and previously Zimbabwe. The U.S. _____ is the official currency of East Timor, Ecuador, El Salvador, Federated States of Micronesia, Marshall Islands, Palau, the Caribbean Netherlands, and for banknotes, Panama. Generally, one _____ is divided into one hundred cents.

    a. Dollar
    b. Bar Kochba Revolt coinage
    c. Bon
    d. British Numismatic Society

2. _____, a portmanteau of stagnation and inflation, is a term used in economics to describe a situation where the inflation rate is high, the economic growth rate slows down, and unemployment remains steadily high. It raises a dilemma for economic policy since actions designed to lower inflation may exacerbate unemployment, and vice versa.

    The term is generally attributed to a British politician who became chancellor of the exchequer in 1970, Iain Macleod, who coined the phrase in his speech to Parliament in 1965.

    In the version of Keynesian macroeconomic theory which was dominant between the end of WWII and the late-1970s, inflation and recession were regarded as mutually exclusive, the relationship between the two being described by the Phillips curve.

    a. Branch plant economy
    b. Capital
    c. Stagflation
    d. Capitalist mode of production

3. In economics, a _____ is a factor of proportionality that measures how much an endogenous variable changes in response to a change in some exogenous variable.

    For example, suppose variable x changes by 1 unit, which causes another variable y to change by M units. Then the _____ is M.

    a. Multiplier
    b. Bureau de change
    c. Business cycle accounting
    d. Classical dichotomy

4. . The general _____ is a hypothetical measure of overall prices for some set of goods and services, in a given region during a given interval, normalized relative to some base set. Typically, a _____ is approximated with a price index.

    a. Break-even
    b. Broad money
    c. Cambridge equation

10. Aggregate Supply and Aggregate Demand

CHAPTER QUIZ: KEY TERMS, PEOPLE, PLACES, CONCEPTS

5. In economics, _____ for a good or service is an entire listing of the quantity of the good or service that a market would choose to buy, for every possible market price of the good or service. (Note: This distinguishes '_____' from 'quantity demanded', where _____ is a listing or graphing of quantity demanded at each possible price. In contrast to _____, quantity demanded is the exact quantity demanded at a certain price.

a. Bad bank
b. Demand
c. Bundism
d. Communist Bund

ANSWER KEY
10. Aggregate Supply and Aggregate Demand

1. a
2. c
3. a
4. d
5. b

You can take the complete Online Interactive Chapter Practice Test

for 10. Aggregate Supply and Aggregate Demand
on all key terms, persons, places, and concepts.

No Additional Costs

http://www.Cram101.com

Register, send an email request to Travis.Reese@Cram101.com to get your user Id and password.

Include your customer order number, and ISBN number from your studyguide Retailer.

11. Expenditure Multipliers

CHAPTER OUTLINE: KEY TERMS, PEOPLE, PLACES, CONCEPTS

- Aggregate expenditure
- Autonomous consumption
- Consumption function
- Fixed price
- Real GDP
- Consumption
- Deflator
- Index
- Price
- Saving
- Dissaving
- Marginal propensity to consume
- Marginal propensity to save
- Marginal propensity to import
- Price level
- Money
- Multiplier
- Size
- Income
- Taxes
- Great Depression

11. Expenditure Multipliers
CHAPTER OUTLINE: KEY TERMS, PEOPLE, PLACES, CONCEPTS

	Business cycle
	Point
	Aggregate demand
	Demand
	Demand curve
	Wealth effect
	Long run
	Long
	Short
	Short run
	Gross domestic income
	Gros
	Keynesian economics
	Balanced budget

11. Expenditure Multipliers

CHAPTER HIGHLIGHTS & NOTES: KEY TERMS, PEOPLE, PLACES, CONCEPTS

Aggregate expenditure	In economics, Aggregate Expenditure is a measure of national income. Aggregate Expenditure is defined as the current value of all the finished goods and services in the economy. The aggregate expenditure is thus the sum total of all the expenditures undertaken in the economy by the factors during a given time period.
Autonomous consumption	Autonomous consumption is consumption expenditure that occurs when income levels are zero. Such consumption is considered autonomous of income only when expenditure on these consumables does not vary with changes in income; generally, it may be required to fund necessities and debt obligations. If income levels are actually zero, this consumption counts as dissaving, because it is financed by borrowing or using up savings.
Consumption function	In economics, the consumption function is a single mathematical function used to express consumer spending. It was developed by John Maynard Keynes and detailed most famously in his book The General Theory of Employment, Interest, and Money. The function is used to calculate the amount of total consumption in an economy.
Fixed price	The term fixed price is a phrase used to mean the price of a good or a service is not subject to bargaining. The term commonly indicates that an external agent, such as a merchant or the government, has set a price level, which may not be changed for individual sales. In the case of governments, this may be due to price controls.
Real GDP	Real Gross Domestic Product (real GDP) is a macroeconomic measure of the value of economic output adjusted for price changes . This adjustment transforms the money-value measure, nominal GDP, into an index for quantity of total output. GDP is the sum of consumer Spending, Investment made by industry, Excess of Exports over Imports and Government Spending.
Consumption	Consumption is a major concept in economics and is also studied by many other social sciences. Economists are particularly interested in the relationship between consumption and income, and therefore in economics the consumption function plays a major role. Different schools of economists define production and consumption differently.
Deflator	In statistics, a deflator is a value that allows data to be measured over time in terms of some base period, usually through a price index, in order to distinguish between a changes in the money value of a gross national product that come from a change in prices, and changes from a change in physical output. It is the measure of the price level for some quantity. A deflator serves as a price index in which the effects of inflation are nulled.
Index	In economics and finance, an index is a statistical measure of changes in a representative group of individual data points. These data may be derived from any number of sources, including company performance, prices, productivity, and employment. Economic indices (index, plural) track economic health from different perspectives.

11. Expenditure Multipliers

CHAPTER HIGHLIGHTS & NOTES: KEY TERMS, PEOPLE, PLACES, CONCEPTS

Price	In ordinary usage, price is the quantity of payment or compensation given by one party to another in return for goods or services.
	In modern economies, prices are generally expressed in units of some form of currency. (For commodities, they are expressed as currency per unit weight of the commodity, e.g. euros per kilogram).
Saving	Saving is income not spent, or deferred consumption. Methods of saving include putting money aside in a bank or pension plan. Saving also includes reducing expenditures, such as recurring costs.
Dissaving	Dissaving is negative saving. If spending is greater than income, dissaving is taking place. This spending is financed by already accumulated savings, such as money in a savings account, or it can be borrowed.
Marginal propensity to consume	In economics, the marginal propensity to consume is a metric that quantifies induced consumption, the concept that the increase in personal consumer spending (consumption) occurs with an increase in disposable income (income after taxes and transfers). The proportion of disposable income which individuals spend on consumption is known as propensity to consume. MPC is the proportion of additional income that an individual consumes.
Marginal propensity to save	The marginal propensity to save refers to the increase in saving (non-purchase of current goods and services) that results from an increase in income i.e. The marginal propensity to save might be defined as the proportion of each additional dollar of household income that is used for saving. It is also used as an alternative term for the slope of the saving line. For example, if a household earns one extra dollar, and the marginal propensity to save is 0.35, then of that dollar, the household will spend 65 cents and save 35 cents.
Marginal propensity to import	The marginal propensity to import refers to the change in import expenditure that occurs with a change in disposable income (income after taxes and transfers). For example, if a household earns one extra dollar of disposable income, and the marginal propensity to import is 0.2, then of that dollar, the household will spend 20 cents of that dollar on imported goods and services.
	Mathematically, the marginal propensity to import function is expressed as the derivative of the import (I) function with respect to disposable income (Y).
Price level	The general price level is a hypothetical measure of overall prices for some set of goods and services, in a given region during a given interval, normalized relative to some base set. Typically, a price level is approximated with a price index.
Money	Monetary disequilibrium theory is basically a product of the Monetarist school mainly represented in the works of Leland Yeager and Austrian macroeconomics.

11. Expenditure Multipliers

CHAPTER HIGHLIGHTS & NOTES: KEY TERMS, PEOPLE, PLACES, CONCEPTS

	The basic concept of monetary equilibrium (disequilibrium) was, however, defined in terms of an individual's demand for cash balance by Mises (1912) in his Theory of Money and Credit.
	Monetary Disequilibrium is one of three theories of macroeconomic fluctuations which accord an important role to money, the others being the Austrian theory of the business cycle and one based on rational expectations.
Multiplier	In economics, a multiplier is a factor of proportionality that measures how much an endogenous variable changes in response to a change in some exogenous variable.
	For example, suppose variable x changes by 1 unit, which causes another variable y to change by M units. Then the multiplier is M.
Size	In statistics, the size of a test is the probability of falsely rejecting the null hypothesis. It is denoted by the Greek letter a (alpha). For a simple hypothesis, $\alpha = P(\text{test rejects } H_0 \vert H_0)$.
	In the case of a composite null hypothesis, the size is the supremum over all null hypotheses.
Income	Income is the consumption and savings opportunity gained by an entity within a specified timeframe, which is generally expressed in monetary terms. However, for households and individuals, 'income is the sum of all the wages, salaries, profits, interests payments, rents and other forms of earnings received... in a given period of time.'
	In the field of public economics, the term may refer to the accumulation of both monetary and non-monetary consumption ability, with the former (monetary) being used as a proxy for total income.
Taxes	A tax is a financial charge or other levy imposed upon a taxpayer (an individual or legal entity) by a state or the functional equivalent of a state such that failure to pay is punishable by law. Taxes are also imposed by many administrative divisions. Taxes consist of direct or indirect taxes and may be paid in money or as its labour equivalent.
Great Depression	The Great Depression was a severe worldwide economic depression in the decade preceding World War II. The timing of the Great Depression varied across nations, but in most countries it started in 1930 and lasted until the late 1930s or middle 1940s. It was the longest, deepest, and most widespread depression of the 20th century.
	In the 21st century, the Great Depression is commonly used as an example of how far the world's economy can decline.
Business cycle	The term business cycle refers to economy-wide fluctuations in production, trade and economic activity in general over several months or years in an economy organized on free-enterprise principles.

11. Expenditure Multipliers

CHAPTER HIGHLIGHTS & NOTES: KEY TERMS, PEOPLE, PLACES, CONCEPTS

	The business cycle is the upward and downward movements of levels of GDP (gross domestic product) and refers to the period of expansions and contractions in the level of economic activities (business fluctuations) around its long-term growth trend. These fluctuations occur around a long-term growth trend, and typically involve shifts over time between periods of relatively rapid economic growth (an expansion or boom), and periods of relative stagnation or decline (a contraction or recession).
Point	Points, sometimes also called 'discount points', are a form of pre-paid interest. One point equals one percent of the loan amount. By charging a borrower points, a lender effectively increases the yield on the loan above the amount of the stated interest rate.
Aggregate demand	In economics, aggregate behavior refers to relationships between economic aggregates such as national income, government expenditure and aggregate demand. For example, the consumption function is a relationship between aggregate demand for consumption and aggregate disposable income. Models of aggregate behavior may be derived from direct observation of the economy, or from models of individual behavior.
Demand	In economics, demand for a good or service is an entire listing of the quantity of the good or service that a market would choose to buy, for every possible market price of the good or service. (Note: This distinguishes 'demand' from 'quantity demanded', where demand is a listing or graphing of quantity demanded at each possible price. In contrast to demand, quantity demanded is the exact quantity demanded at a certain price.
Demand curve	In economics, the demand curve is the graph depicting the relationship between the price of a certain commodity and the amount of it that consumers are willing and able to purchase at that given price. It is a graphic representation of a demand schedule. The demand curve for all consumers together follows from the demand curve of every individual consumer: the individual demands at each price are added together.
Wealth effect	The wealth effect is an economic term, referring to an increase in spending that accompanies an increase (decrease) in perceived wealth.
Long run	In microeconomics, the long run is the conceptual time period in which there are no fixed factors of production as to changing the output level by changing the capital stock or by entering or leaving an industry. The long run contrasts with the short run, in which some factors are variable and others are fixed, constraining entry or exit from an industry.

11. Expenditure Multipliers

CHAPTER HIGHLIGHTS & NOTES: KEY TERMS, PEOPLE, PLACES, CONCEPTS

Long	Long/short equity is an investment strategy generally associated with hedge funds, and more recently certain progressive traditional asset managers. It involves buying long equities that are expected to increase in value and selling short equities that are expected to decrease in value. This is different from the risk reversal strategies where investors will simultaneously buy a call option and sell a put option to simulate being long in a stock.
Short	In finance, short selling (also known as shorting or going short) is the practice of selling securities or other financial instruments that are not currently owned, and subsequently repurchasing them . In the event of an interim price decline, the short seller will profit, since the cost of (re)purchase will be less than the proceeds which were received upon the initial (short) sale. Conversely, the short position will be closed out at a loss in the event that the price of a shorted instrument should rise prior to repurchase.
Short run	In microeconomics, the long run is the conceptual time period in which there are no fixed factors of production, so that there are no constraints preventing changing the output level by changing the capital stock or by entering or leaving an industry. The long run contrasts with the short run, in which some factors are variable and others are fixed, constraining entry or exit from an industry. In macroeconomics, the long run is the period when the general price level, contractual wage rates, and expectations adjust fully to the state of the economy, in contrast to the short run when these variables may not fully adjust.
Gross domestic income	The Gross Domestic Income is the total income received by all sectors of an economy within a State. It includes the sum of all wages, profits, and taxes, minus subsidies. Since all income is derived from production (including the production of services), the gross domestic income of a country should exactly equal its gross domestic product (GDP).
Gros	A gros was a type of silver coinage of France from the time of Saint Louis. There were gros tournois and gros parisis. The gros was sub-divided in half gros and quarter gros.
Keynesian economics	Keynesian economics is the view that in the short run, especially during recessions, economic output is strongly influenced by aggregate demand (total spending in the economy). In the Keynesian view, aggregate demand does not necessarily equal the productive capacity of the economy; instead, it is influenced by a host of factors and sometimes behaves erratically, affecting production, employment, and inflation. The theories forming the basis of Keynesian economics were first presented by the British economist John Maynard Keynes in his book, The General Theory of Employment, Interest and Money, published in 1936, during the Great Depression.
Balanced budget	A balanced budget refers to a budget in which revenues are equal to expenditures. Thus, neither a budget deficit nor a budget surplus exists ('the accounts balance').

11. Expenditure Multipliers

CHAPTER QUIZ: KEY TERMS, PEOPLE, PLACES, CONCEPTS

1. The general _____ is a hypothetical measure of overall prices for some set of goods and services, in a given region during a given interval, normalized relative to some base set. Typically, a _____ is approximated with a price index.

   a. Break-even
   b. Broad money
   c. Cambridge equation
   d. Price level

2. In economics, the _____ is a metric that quantifies induced consumption, the concept that the increase in personal consumer spending (consumption) occurs with an increase in disposable income (income after taxes and transfers). The proportion of disposable income which individuals spend on consumption is known as propensity to consume. MPC is the proportion of additional income that an individual consumes.

   a. Ricardian equivalence
   b. Boukaseff scale
   c. Marginal propensity to consume
   d. Business cycle accounting

3. In statistics, a _____ is a value that allows data to be measured over time in terms of some base period, usually through a price index, in order to distinguish between a changes in the money value of a gross national product that come from a change in prices, and changes from a change in physical output. It is the measure of the price level for some quantity. A _____ serves as a price index in which the effects of inflation are nulled.

   a. Binary data
   b. Deflator
   c. Cause of death
   d. Ceiling effect

4. In economics, the _____ is a single mathematical function used to express consumer spending. It was developed by John Maynard Keynes and detailed most famously in his book The General Theory of Employment, Interest, and Money. The function is used to calculate the amount of total consumption in an economy.

   a. Boukaseff scale
   b. Bureau de change
   c. Consumption function
   d. Classical dichotomy

5. . In economics, _____ is a measure of national income. _____ is defined as the current value of all the finished goods and services in the economy. The _____ is thus the sum total of all the expenditures undertaken in the economy by the factors during a given time period.

   a. Federal Reserve
   b. Fuel protests in the United Kingdom
   c. 2010 student protest in Dublin

ANSWER KEY
11. Expenditure Multipliers

1. d
2. c
3. b
4. c
5. d

You can take the complete Online Interactive Chapter Practice Test

for 11. Expenditure Multipliers
on all key terms, persons, places, and concepts.

No Additional Costs

http://www.Cram101.com

Register, send an email request to Travis.Reese@Cram101.com to get your user Id and password.

Include your customer order number, and ISBN number from your studyguide Retailer.

12. The Business Cycle, Inflation, and Deflation

CHAPTER OUTLINE: KEY TERMS, PEOPLE, PLACES, CONCEPTS

- Business cycle
- Long
- New Keynesian
- Total factor productivity
- Labor force
- Rate
- Aggregate demand
- Demand-pull inflation
- JPMorgan Chase
- Inflation
- Money
- Multiplier
- Wage
- Cost-push inflation
- Price
- Price level
- Stagflation
- Forecasting
- Quantitative easing
- Deflation
- Exchange

12. The Business Cycle, Inflation, and Deflation
CHAPTER OUTLINE: KEY TERMS, PEOPLE, PLACES, CONCEPTS

	Quantity theory
	Personal consumption
	Phillips curve
	European Central Bank
	Eurozone
	Unemployment
	Tariff
	Trade

CHAPTER HIGHLIGHTS & NOTES: KEY TERMS, PEOPLE, PLACES, CONCEPTS

Business cycle	The term business cycle refers to economy-wide fluctuations in production, trade and economic activity in general over several months or years in an economy organized on free-enterprise principles. The business cycle is the upward and downward movements of levels of GDP (gross domestic product) and refers to the period of expansions and contractions in the level of economic activities (business fluctuations) around its long-term growth trend. These fluctuations occur around a long-term growth trend, and typically involve shifts over time between periods of relatively rapid economic growth (an expansion or boom), and periods of relative stagnation or decline (a contraction or recession).
Long	Long/short equity is an investment strategy generally associated with hedge funds, and more recently certain progressive traditional asset managers. It involves buying long equities that are expected to increase in value and selling short equities that are expected to decrease in value. This is different from the risk reversal strategies where investors will simultaneously buy a call option and sell a put option to simulate being long in a stock.

12. The Business Cycle, Inflation, and Deflation

CHAPTER HIGHLIGHTS & NOTES: KEY TERMS, PEOPLE, PLACES, CONCEPTS

New Keynesian	New Keynesian economics is a school of contemporary macroeconomics that strives to provide microeconomic foundations for Keynesian economics. It developed partly as a response to criticisms of Keynesian macroeconomics by adherents of New Classical macroeconomics. Two main assumptions define the New Keynesian approach to macroeconomics.
Total factor productivity	In economics, total-factor productivity, also called multi-factor productivity, is a variable which accounts for effects in total output not caused by traditionally measured inputs of labor and capital. If all inputs are accounted for, then total factor productivity can be taken as a measure of an economy's long-term technological change or technological dynamism. Total factor productivity cannot be measured directly.
Labor force	The labor force is the actual number of people available for work. The labor force of a country includes both the employed and the unemployed. The labor force participation rate, LFPR (or economic activity rate, EAR), is the ratio between the labor force and the overall size of their cohort (national population of the same age range).
Rate	In mathematics, a rate is a ratio between two measurements with different units. If the unit or quantity in respect of which something is changing is not specified, usually the rate is per unit time. However, a rate of change can be specified per unit time, or per unit of length or mass or another quantity.
Aggregate demand	In economics, aggregate behavior refers to relationships between economic aggregates such as national income, government expenditure and aggregate demand. For example, the consumption function is a relationship between aggregate demand for consumption and aggregate disposable income. Models of aggregate behavior may be derived from direct observation of the economy, or from models of individual behavior.
Demand-pull inflation	Demand-pull inflation is asserted to arise when aggregate demand in an economy outpaces aggregate supply. It involves inflation rising as real gross domestic product rises and unemployment falls, as the economy moves along the Phillips curve. This is commonly described as 'too much money chasing too few goods'.
JPMorgan Chase	JPMorgan Chase & Co. is an American multinational banking and financial services holding company. It is the largest bank in the United States, with total assets of US$2.415 trillion. It is a major provider of financial services, and according to Forbes magazine is the world's third largest public company based on a composite ranking.

12. The Business Cycle, Inflation, and Deflation

CHAPTER HIGHLIGHTS & NOTES: KEY TERMS, PEOPLE, PLACES, CONCEPTS

Inflation	In economics, inflation is a sustained increase in the general price level of goods and services in an economy over a period of time. When the general price level rises, each unit of currency buys fewer goods and services. Consequently, inflation reflects a reduction in the purchasing power per unit of money - a loss of real value in the medium of exchange and unit of account within the economy.
Money	Monetary disequilibrium theory is basically a product of the Monetarist school mainly represented in the works of Leland Yeager and Austrian macroeconomics. The basic concept of monetary equilibrium (disequilibrium) was, however, defined in terms of an individual's demand for cash balance by Mises (1912) in his Theory of Money and Credit. Monetary Disequilibrium is one of three theories of macroeconomic fluctuations which accord an important role to money, the others being the Austrian theory of the business cycle and one based on rational expectations.
Multiplier	In economics, a multiplier is a factor of proportionality that measures how much an endogenous variable changes in response to a change in some exogenous variable. For example, suppose variable x changes by 1 unit, which causes another variable y to change by M units. Then the multiplier is M.
Wage	A wage is monetary compensation paid by an employer to an employee in exchange for work done. Payment may be calculated as a fixed amount for each task completed (a task wage or piece rate), or at an hourly or daily rate, or based on an easily measured quantity of work done. Payment by wage contrasts with salaried work, in which the employer pays an arranged amount at steady intervals (such as a week or month) regardless of hours worked, with commission which conditions pay on individual performance, and with compensation based on the performance of the company as a whole.
Cost-push inflation	Cost-push inflation is an alleged type of inflation caused by substantial increases in the cost of important goods or services where no suitable alternative is available. A situation that has been often cited of this was the oil crisis of the 1970s, which some economists see as a major cause of the inflation experienced in the Western world in that decade. It is argued that this inflation resulted from increases in the cost of petroleum imposed by the member states of OPEC. Since petroleum is so important to industrialised economies, a large increase in its price can lead to the increase in the price of most products, raising the inflation rate.
Price	In ordinary usage, price is the quantity of payment or compensation given by one party to another in return for goods or services. In modern economies, prices are generally expressed in units of some form of currency.

12. The Business Cycle, Inflation, and Deflation

CHAPTER HIGHLIGHTS & NOTES: KEY TERMS, PEOPLE, PLACES, CONCEPTS

	(For commodities, they are expressed as currency per unit weight of the commodity, e.g. euros per kilogram).
Price level	The general price level is a hypothetical measure of overall prices for some set of goods and services, in a given region during a given interval, normalized relative to some base set. Typically, a price level is approximated with a price index.
Stagflation	Stagflation, a portmanteau of stagnation and inflation, is a term used in economics to describe a situation where the inflation rate is high, the economic growth rate slows down, and unemployment remains steadily high. It raises a dilemma for economic policy since actions designed to lower inflation may exacerbate unemployment, and vice versa. The term is generally attributed to a British politician who became chancellor of the exchequer in 1970, Iain Macleod, who coined the phrase in his speech to Parliament in 1965. In the version of Keynesian macroeconomic theory which was dominant between the end of WWII and the late-1970s, inflation and recession were regarded as mutually exclusive, the relationship between the two being described by the Phillips curve.
Forecasting	Forecasting is the process of making statements about events whose actual outcomes have not yet been observed. A commonplace example might be estimation of some variable of interest at some specified future date. Prediction is a similar, but more general term.
Quantitative easing	Quantitative easing is an unconventional monetary policy used by central banks to stimulate the economy when standard monetary policy has become ineffective. A central bank implements quantitative easing by buying specified amounts of financial assets from commercial banks and other private institutions, thus raising the prices of those financial assets and lowering their yield, while simultaneously increasing the monetary base. This is distinguished from the more usual policy of buying or selling short term government bonds in order to keep interbank interest rates at a specified target value.
Deflation	In economics, deflation is a decrease in the general price level of goods and services. Deflation occurs when the inflation rate falls below 0% (a negative inflation rate). This should not be confused with disinflation, a slow-down in the inflation rate (i.e., when inflation declines to lower levels).
Exchange	An exchange, or bourse, is a highly organized market where tradable securities, commodities, foreign exchange, futures, and options contracts are sold and bought.
Quantity theory	In monetary economics, the quantity theory of money states that money supply has a direct, proportional relationship with the price level. While mainstream economists agree that the quantity theory holds true in the long run, there is still disagreement about its applicability in the short run.

12. The Business Cycle, Inflation, and Deflation

CHAPTER HIGHLIGHTS & NOTES: KEY TERMS, PEOPLE, PLACES, CONCEPTS

Personal consumption	The Personal Consumption Expenditure measure is the component statistic for consumption in GDP collected by the BEA. It consists of the actual and imputed expenditures of households and includes data pertaining to durable and non-durable goods and services. It is essentially a measure of goods and services targeted towards individuals and consumed by individuals. The PCE price index (PCEPI), also referred to as the PCE deflator, PCE price deflator, or the Implicit Price Deflator for Personal Consumption Expenditures (IPD for PCE) by the BEA, and as the Chain-type Price Index for Personal Consumption Expenditures (CTPIPCE) by the FOMC, is a United States-wide indicator of the average increase in prices for all domestic personal consumption.
Phillips curve	In economics, the Phillips curve is a historical inverse relationship between rates of unemployment and corresponding rates of inflation that result in an economy. Stated simply, decreased unemployment, (i.e., increased levels of employment) in an economy will correlate with higher rates of inflation. While there is a short run tradeoff between unemployment and inflation, it has not been observed in the long run.
European Central Bank	The European Central Bank is the central bank for the euro and administers the monetary policy of the Eurozone, which consists of 18 EU member states and is one of the largest currency areas in the world. It is one of the world's most important central banks and is one of the seven institutions of the European Union (EU) listed in the Treaty on European Union (TEU). The capital stock of the bank is owned by the central banks of all 28 EU member states.
Eurozone	The eurozone, officially called the euro area, is a monetary union of 19 European Union (EU) member states that have adopted the euro (€) as their common currency and sole legal tender. The eurozone consists of Austria, Belgium, Cyprus, Estonia, Finland, France, Germany, Greece, Ireland, Italy, Latvia, Lithuania, Luxembourg, Malta, the Netherlands, Portugal, Slovakia, Slovenia, and Spain. Other EU states (except for Denmark and the United Kingdom) are obliged to join once they meet the criteria to do so.
Unemployment	Unemployment occurs when people are without work and actively seeking work. The unemployment rate is a measure of the prevalence of unemployment and it is calculated as a percentage by dividing the number of unemployed individuals by all individuals currently in the labor force. During periods of recession, an economy usually experiences a relatively high unemployment rate.
Tariff	A tariff is a tax on imports or exports (an international trade tariff), or a list of prices for such things as rail service, bus routes, and electrical usage (electrical tariff, etc).. The meaning in (1) is now the more common meaning.

12. The Business Cycle, Inflation, and Deflation

CHAPTER HIGHLIGHTS & NOTES: KEY TERMS, PEOPLE, PLACES, CONCEPTS

Trade	In finance, a trade is an exchange of a security for 'cash', typically a short-dated promise to pay in the currency of the country where the 'exchange' is located.

CHAPTER QUIZ: KEY TERMS, PEOPLE, PLACES, CONCEPTS

1. In economics, a _____ is a factor of proportionality that measures how much an endogenous variable changes in response to a change in some exogenous variable.

   For example, suppose variable x changes by 1 unit, which causes another variable y to change by M units. Then the _____ is M.

   a. Boukaseff scale
   b. Bureau de change
   c. Business cycle accounting
   d. Multiplier

2. _____ & Co. is an American multinational banking and financial services holding company. It is the largest bank in the United States, with total assets of US$2.415 trillion. It is a major provider of financial services, and according to Forbes magazine is the world's third largest public company based on a composite ranking.

   a. Bank of America
   b. JPMorgan Chase
   c. Barclays Investment Bank
   d. BNP Paribas CIB

3. . The term _____ refers to economy-wide fluctuations in production, trade and economic activity in general over several months or years in an economy organized on free-enterprise principles.

   The _____ is the upward and downward movements of levels of GDP (gross domestic product) and refers to the period of expansions and contractions in the level of economic activities (business fluctuations) around its long-term growth trend.

   These fluctuations occur around a long-term growth trend, and typically involve shifts over time between periods of relatively rapid economic growth (an expansion or boom), and periods of relative stagnation or decline (a contraction or recession).

   a. Bad bank
   b. Bank failure
   c. Jewish Social Democratic Party

12. The Business Cycle, Inflation, and Deflation

CHAPTER QUIZ: KEY TERMS, PEOPLE, PLACES, CONCEPTS

4. In finance, a _____ is an exchange of a security for 'cash', typically a short-dated promise to pay in the currency of the country where the 'exchange' is located.

   a. Bagholder
   b. Trade
   c. BATS Chi-X Europe
   d. Bear raid

5. _____/short equity is an investment strategy generally associated with hedge funds, and more recently certain progressive traditional asset managers. It involves buying _____ equities that are expected to increase in value and selling short equities that are expected to decrease in value. This is different from the risk reversal strategies where investors will simultaneously buy a call option and sell a put option to simulate being _____ in a stock.

   a. Clearing
   b. Financial market
   c. Long
   d. Bad bank

ANSWER KEY
12. The Business Cycle, Inflation, and Deflation

1. d
2. b
3. d
4. b
5. c

You can take the complete Online Interactive Chapter Practice Test

for 12. The Business Cycle, Inflation, and Deflation
on all key terms, persons, places, and concepts.

No Additional Costs

http://www.Cram101.com

Register, send an email request to Travis.Reese@Cram101.com to get your user Id and password.

Include your customer order number, and ISBN number from your studyguide Retailer.

13. Fiscal Policy

CHAPTER OUTLINE: KEY TERMS, PEOPLE, PLACES, CONCEPTS

	Federal budget
	Fiscal policy
	Great Depression
	Institution
	Economic Report of the President
	Indirect tax
	Social Security
	Transfer payment
	Taxes
	Balanced budget
	Budget deficit
	Good
	Debt
	Interest
	Perspective
	Service
	Government debt
	Capital
	Government budget
	Full employment
	Income

13. Fiscal Policy
CHAPTER OUTLINE: KEY TERMS, PEOPLE, PLACES, CONCEPTS

	Supply-side
	Tax wedge
	Deflator
	Interest rate
	Investment
	Saving
	Laffer curve
	Baby boomers
	Fiscal imbalance
	Generational accounting
	Medicare
	New Deal
	Present value
	Generational imbalance
	Tax revenue
	Congressional Budget Office
	Recessionary gap
	Balance
	Aggregate demand
	Demand
	Multiplier

13. Fiscal Policy

CHAPTER OUTLINE: KEY TERMS, PEOPLE, PLACES, CONCEPTS

	Stimulus
	Aggregate supply
	Supply

CHAPTER HIGHLIGHTS & NOTES: KEY TERMS, PEOPLE, PLACES, CONCEPTS

Federal budget	In economics, a federal budget is a plan for the Federal government's revenues and spending for the coming year.
Fiscal policy	In economics and political science, fiscal policy is the use of government revenue collection and expenditure (spending) to influence the economy. The two main instruments of fiscal policy are changes in the level and composition of taxation and government spending in various sectors. These changes can affect the following macroeconomic variables in an economy:•Aggregate demand and the level of economic activity;•The distribution of income;•The pattern of resource allocation within the government sector and relative to the private sector. Fiscal policy refers to the use of the government budget to influence economic activity.
Great Depression	The Great Depression was a severe worldwide economic depression in the decade preceding World War II. The timing of the Great Depression varied across nations, but in most countries it started in 1930 and lasted until the late 1930s or middle 1940s. It was the longest, deepest, and most widespread depression of the 20th century. In the 21st century, the Great Depression is commonly used as an example of how far the world's economy can decline.
Institution	An institution is any structure or mechanism of social order governing the behaviour of a set of individuals within a given community; may it be human or a specific animal one. Institutions are identified with a social purpose, transcending individuals and intentions by mediating the rules that govern living behavior. The term 'institution' is commonly applied to customs and behavior patterns important to a society, as well as to particular formal organizations of government and public services.

13. Fiscal Policy

CHAPTER HIGHLIGHTS & NOTES: KEY TERMS, PEOPLE, PLACES, CONCEPTS

Economic Report of the President	The Economic Report of the President is a document published by the President of the United States' Council of Economic Advisers . Released in February of each year, the report reviews what economic activity was of impact in the previous year, outlines the economic goals for the coming year (based on the President's economic agenda), and makes numerical projections of how the economy will perform. Criticism usually follows, sometimes attacking the importance placed or not placed on particular data, and also on the importance of particular goals presented in the Overview.
Indirect tax	An indirect tax (such as sales tax, a specific tax, value added tax, or goods and services tax (GST)) is a tax collected by an intermediary (such as a retail store) from the person who bears the ultimate economic burden of the tax (such as the consumer). The intermediary later files a tax return and forwards the tax proceeds to government with the return. In this sense, the term indirect tax is contrasted with a direct tax which is collected directly by government from the persons (legal or natural) on which it is imposed.
Social Security	In the United States, Social Security is primarily the Old-Age, Survivors, and Disability Insurance federal program. The original Social Security Act (1935) and the current version of the Act, as amended, encompass several social welfare and social insurance programs. Social Security is funded through payroll taxes called Federal Insurance Contributions Act tax (FICA) and/or Self Employed Contributions Act Tax (SECA).
Transfer payment	In economics, a transfer payment is a redistribution of income in the market system. These payments are considered to be non-exhaustive because they do not directly absorb resources or create output. In other words, the transfer is made without any exchange of goods or services.
Taxes	A tax is a financial charge or other levy imposed upon a taxpayer (an individual or legal entity) by a state or the functional equivalent of a state such that failure to pay is punishable by law. Taxes are also imposed by many administrative divisions. Taxes consist of direct or indirect taxes and may be paid in money or as its labour equivalent.
Balanced budget	A balanced budget refers to a budget in which revenues are equal to expenditures. Thus, neither a budget deficit nor a budget surplus exists ('the accounts balance'). More generally, it refers to a budget that has no budget deficit, but could possibly have a budget surplus.
Budget deficit	A government budget is a government document presenting the government's proposed revenues and spending for a financial year. The government budget balance, also alternatively referred to as general government balance, public budget balance, or public fiscal balance, is the overall difference between government revenues and spending. A positive balance is called a government budget surplus, and a negative balance is a government budget deficit.
Good	In economics, a good is a material that satisfies human wants and provides utility, for example, to a consumer making a purchase. A common distinction is made between 'goods' that are tangible property (also called goods) and services, which are non-physical.

13. Fiscal Policy

CHAPTER HIGHLIGHTS & NOTES: KEY TERMS, PEOPLE, PLACES, CONCEPTS

Debt	A debt is an obligation owed by one party (the debtor) to a second party, the creditor; usually this refers to assets granted by the creditor to the debtor, but the term can also be used metaphorically to cover moral obligations and other interactions not based on economic value. A debt is created when a creditor agrees to lend a sum of assets to a debtor. Debt is usually granted with expected repayment; in modern society, in most cases, this includes repayment of the original sum, plus interest.
Interest	Interest is a fee paid by a borrower of assets to the owner as a form of compensation for the use of the assets. It is most commonly the price paid for the use of borrowed money, or money earned by deposited funds. When money is borrowed, interest is typically paid to the lender as a percentage of the principal, the amount owed to the lender.
Perspective	Perspective in pharmacoeconomics refers to the economic vantage point of a pharmacoeconomic analysis, such as a cost-effectiveness analysis or cost-utility analysis. This affects the types of costs (resource expenditures) and benefits that are relevant to the analysis. Five general perspectives are often cited in pharmacoeconomics, including institutional, third party, patient, governmental and societal.
Service	In economics, a service is an intangible commodity. That is, services are an example of intangible economic goods. Service provision is often an economic activity where the buyer does not generally, except by exclusive contract, obtain exclusive ownership of the thing purchased.
Government debt	Government debt is the debt owed by a central government. (In the U.S. and other federal states, 'government debt' may also refer to the debt of a state or provincial government, municipal or local government). By contrast, the annual 'government deficit' refers to the difference between government receipts and spending in a single year, that is, the increase of debt over a particular year.
Capital	In economics, capital goods, real capital, or capital assets are already-produced durable goods or any non-financial asset that is used in production of goods or services. Capital goods are not significantly consumed in the production process though they may depreciate. How a capital good or is maintained or returned to its pre-production state varies with the type of capital involved.

13. Fiscal Policy

CHAPTER HIGHLIGHTS & NOTES: KEY TERMS, PEOPLE, PLACES, CONCEPTS

Government budget	A government budget is a government document presenting the government's proposed revenues and spending for a financial year that is often passed by the legislature, approved by the chief executive or president and presented by the Finance Minister to the nation. The budget is also known as the Annual Financial Statement of the country. This document estimates the anticipated government revenues and government expenditures for the ensuing (current) financial year.
Full employment	Full employment, in macroeconomics, is the level of employment rates where there is no cyclical or deficient-demand unemployment. It is defined by the majority of mainstream economists as being an acceptable level of unemployment somewhere above 0%. The discrepancy from 0% arises due to non-cyclical types of unemployment.
Income	Income is the consumption and savings opportunity gained by an entity within a specified timeframe, which is generally expressed in monetary terms. However, for households and individuals, 'income is the sum of all the wages, salaries, profits, interests payments, rents and other forms of earnings received... in a given period of time.' In the field of public economics, the term may refer to the accumulation of both monetary and non-monetary consumption ability, with the former (monetary) being used as a proxy for total income.
Supply-side	Supply-side economics is a school of macroeconomics that argues that economic growth can be most effectively created by lowering barriers for people to produce goods and services as well as invest in capital. According to supply-side economics, consumers will then benefit from a greater supply of goods and services at lower prices; furthermore, the investment and expansion of businesses will increase the demand for employees. Typical policy recommendations of supply-side economists are lower marginal tax rates and less regulation.
Tax wedge	The tax wedge is the deviation from equilibrium price/quantity as a result of a taxation, which results in consumers paying more, and suppliers receiving less. Following from the Law of Supply and Demand, as the price to consumers increases, and the price suppliers receive decreases, the quantity each wishes to trade will decrease. After a tax is introduced, a new equilibrium is reached where consumers pay more (P* ? Pc), suppliers receive less (P* ? Ps), and the quantity exchanged falls (Q* ? Qt).
Deflator	In statistics, a deflator is a value that allows data to be measured over time in terms of some base period, usually through a price index, in order to distinguish between a changes in the money value of a gross national product that come from a change in prices, and changes from a change in physical output. It is the measure of the price level for some quantity. A deflator serves as a price index in which the effects of inflation are nulled.
Interest rate	An interest rate is the rate at which interest is paid by a borrower for the use of money that they borrow from a lender (creditor).

13. Fiscal Policy

CHAPTER HIGHLIGHTS & NOTES: KEY TERMS, PEOPLE, PLACES, CONCEPTS

	Specifically, the interest rate is a percent of principal (P) paid a certain amount of times (m) per period (usually quoted per annum). For example, a small company borrows capital from a bank to buy new assets for its business, and in return the lender receives interest at a predetermined interest rate for deferring the use of funds and instead lending it to the borrower.
Investment	Investment is time, energy, or matter spent in the hope of future benefits. Investment has different meanings in economics and finance. In economics, investment is the accumulation of newly produced physical entities, such as factories, machinery, houses, and goods inventories.
Saving	Saving is income not spent, or deferred consumption. Methods of saving include putting money aside in a bank or pension plan. Saving also includes reducing expenditures, such as recurring costs.
Laffer curve	In economics, the Laffer curve is a representation of the relationship between possible rates of taxation and the resulting levels of government revenue. It illustrates the concept of taxable income elasticity--i.e., taxable income will change in response to changes in the rate of taxation. It postulates that no tax revenue will be raised at the extreme tax rates of 0% and 100% and that there must be at least one rate where tax revenue would be a non-zero maximum.
Baby boomers	A baby boom is any period marked by a greatly increased birth rate. This demographic phenomenon is usually ascribed within certain geographical bounds. People born during such a period are often called baby boomers; however, some experts distinguish between those born during such demographic baby booms and those who identify with the overlapping cultural generations.
Fiscal imbalance	Fiscal imbalance is a mismatch in the revenue powers and expenditure responsibilities of a government. In the literature on fiscal federalism, two types of fiscal imbalances are measured: Vertical Fiscal Imbalance and Horizontal Fiscal Imbalance. When the fiscal imbalance is measured between the two levels of government (Center and States or Provinces) it is called Vertical Fiscal Imbalance.
Generational accounting	Generational accounting measures the fiscal burdens facing today's and tomorrow's children. Laurence Kotlikoff's individual and co-authored work on the relativity of fiscal language demonstrates that conventional fiscal measures, including the government's deficit, are not well defined from the perspective of economic theory. Instead, their measurement reflects economically arbitrary fiscal labeling conventions.
Medicare	In the United States, Medicare is a national social insurance program, administered by the U.S.

13. Fiscal Policy

CHAPTER HIGHLIGHTS & NOTES: KEY TERMS, PEOPLE, PLACES, CONCEPTS

	federal government since 1966, that guarantees access to health insurance for Americans aged 65 and older who have worked and paid into the system, and younger people with disabilities as well as people with end stage renal disease (Medicare.gov, 2012) and persons with amyotrophic lateral sclerosis. As a social insurance program, Medicare spreads the financial risk associated with illness across society to protect everyone, and thus has a somewhat different social role from for-profit private insurers, which manage their risk portfolio by adjusting their pricing according to perceived risk. In 2010, Medicare provided health insurance to 48 million Americans--40 million people age 65 and older and eight million younger people with disabilities.
New Deal	The New Deal was a series of domestic programs enacted in the United States between 1933 and 1936, and a few that came later. They included both laws passed by Congress as well as presidential executive orders during the first term (1933-37) of President Franklin D. Roosevelt. The programs were in response to the Great Depression, and focused on what historians call the '3 Rs': Relief, Recovery, and Reform.
Present value	Present value, also known as present discounted value, is a future amount of money that has been discounted to reflect its current value, as if it existed today. The present value is always less than or equal to the future value because money has interest-earning potential, a characteristic referred to as the time value of money. Time value can be described with the simplified phrase, "A dollar today is worth more than a dollar tomorrow".
Generational imbalance	Generational imbalance is the economic and political tension which characterizes a state which has a reduced birth rate and increased health resulting in an increasing aging population compared to its younger working population; cost and generosity of welfare systems also plays a role.
Tax revenue	Tax revenue is the income that is gained by governments through taxation. Just as there are different types of tax, the form in which tax revenue is collected also differs; furthermore, the agency that collects the tax may not be part of central government, but may be an alternative third-party licenced to collect tax which they themselves will use. For example:•In the UK, the DVLA collects vehicle excise duty, which is then passed onto the treasury. Tax revenues on purchases can come from two forms: 'tax' itself is a percentage of the price added to the purchase (such as sales tax in US states, or VAT in the UK), while 'duty' is a fixed amount added to the purchase price (such as is commonly found on cigarettes).
Congressional Budget Office	The Congressional Budget Office is a federal agency within the legislative branch of the United States government that provides economic data to Congress. The Congressional Budget Office was created as a nonpartisan agency by the Congressional Budget and Impoundment Control Act of 1974.

13. Fiscal Policy

CHAPTER HIGHLIGHTS & NOTES: KEY TERMS, PEOPLE, PLACES, CONCEPTS

Recessionary gap	The GDP gap or the output gap is the difference between actual GDP or actual output and potential GDP. The calculation for the output gap is Y-Y* where Y is actual output and Y* is potential output. If this calculation yields a positive number it is called an inflationary gap and indicates the growth of aggregate demand is outpacing the growth of aggregate supply--possibly creating inflation; if the calculation yields a negative number it is called a recessionary gap--possibly signifying deflation. The percentage GDP gap is the actual GDP minus the potential GDP divided by the potential GDP. $(GDP_{actual} - GDP_{potential}) / GDP_{potential}$ {displaystyle {(GDP_{actual}-GDP_{potential})} over {GDP_{potential}}}.
Balance	In banking and accountancy, the outstanding balance is the amount of money owed that remains in a deposit account (or a loan account) at a given date, after all past remittances, payments and withdrawal have been accounted for. It can be positive (then, in the balance sheet of a firm, it is an asset) or negative (a liability).
Aggregate demand	In economics, aggregate behavior refers to relationships between economic aggregates such as national income, government expenditure and aggregate demand. For example, the consumption function is a relationship between aggregate demand for consumption and aggregate disposable income. Models of aggregate behavior may be derived from direct observation of the economy, or from models of individual behavior.
Demand	In economics, demand for a good or service is an entire listing of the quantity of the good or service that a market would choose to buy, for every possible market price of the good or service. (Note: This distinguishes 'demand' from 'quantity demanded', where demand is a listing or graphing of quantity demanded at each possible price. In contrast to demand, quantity demanded is the exact quantity demanded at a certain price.
Multiplier	In economics, a multiplier is a factor of proportionality that measures how much an endogenous variable changes in response to a change in some exogenous variable. For example, suppose variable x changes by 1 unit, which causes another variable y to change by M units. Then the multiplier is M.
Stimulus	In economics, stimulus refers to attempts to use monetary or fiscal policy to stimulate the economy. Stimulus can also refer to monetary policies like lowering interest rates and quantitative easing.
Aggregate supply	In economics, aggregate supply is the total supply of goods and services that firms in a national economy plan on selling during a specific time period.

13. Fiscal Policy

CHAPTER HIGHLIGHTS & NOTES: KEY TERMS, PEOPLE, PLACES, CONCEPTS

	It is the total amount of goods and services that firms are willing to sell at a given price level in an economy.
Supply	In economics, supply refers to the amount of a product that producers and firms are willing to sell at a given price all other factors being held constant. Usually, supply is plotted as a supply curve showing the relationship of price to the amount of product businesses are willing to sell.

CHAPTER QUIZ: KEY TERMS, PEOPLE, PLACES, CONCEPTS

1. In the United States, _____ is primarily the Old-Age, Survivors, and Disability Insurance federal program. The original _____ Act (1935) and the current version of the Act, as amended, encompass several social welfare and social insurance programs. _____ is funded through payroll taxes called Federal Insurance Contributions Act tax (FICA) and/or Self Employed Contributions Act Tax (SECA).

   a. Bad bank
   b. Bank failure
   c. Jewish Social Democratic Party
   d. Social Security

2. In economics, aggregate behavior refers to relationships between economic aggregates such as national income, government expenditure and _____. For example, the consumption function is a relationship between _____ for consumption and aggregate disposable income.

   Models of aggregate behavior may be derived from direct observation of the economy, or from models of individual behavior.

   a. Bad bank
   b. Aggregate demand
   c. Jewish Social Democratic Party
   d. Communist Bund

3. The _____ is a federal agency within the legislative branch of the United States government that provides economic data to Congress. The _____ was created as a nonpartisan agency by the Congressional Budget and Impoundment Control Act of 1974.

   a. 1996 United States federal budget
   b. Congressional Budget Office
   c. 2012 United States federal budget
   d. 2013 United States federal budget

13. Fiscal Policy

CHAPTER QUIZ: KEY TERMS, PEOPLE, PLACES, CONCEPTS

4. In economics, a _____ is an intangible commodity. That is, _____s are an example of intangible economic goods.

   _____ provision is often an economic activity where the buyer does not generally, except by exclusive contract, obtain exclusive ownership of the thing purchased.

   a. Base period
   b. Benefit incidence
   c. Blanket order
   d. Service

5. In economics and political science, _____ is the use of government revenue collection and expenditure (spending) to influence the economy. The two main instruments of _____ are changes in the level and composition of taxation and government spending in various sectors. These changes can affect the following macroeconomic variables in an economy:•Aggregate demand and the level of economic activity;•The distribution of income;•The pattern of resource allocation within the government sector and relative to the private sector.

   _____ refers to the use of the government budget to influence economic activity.

   a. Bad bank
   b. Bank failure
   c. Bundism
   d. Fiscal policy

ANSWER KEY
13. Fiscal Policy

1. d
2. b
3. b
4. d
5. d

You can take the complete Online Interactive Chapter Practice Test

for 13. Fiscal Policy
on all key terms, persons, places, and concepts.

No Additional Costs

http://www.Cram101.com

Register, send an email request to Travis.Reese@Cram101.com to get your user Id and password.

Include your customer order number, and ISBN number from your studyguide Retailer.

14. Monetary Policy

CHAPTER OUTLINE: KEY TERMS, PEOPLE, PLACES, CONCEPTS

- _____ Federal Reserve
- _____ Federal Reserve Act
- _____ Monetary policy
- _____ Stability
- _____ Bernanke
- _____ Consumer price index
- _____ Core inflation
- _____ Inflationary gap
- _____ Output gap
- _____ Personal consumption
- _____ Operational
- _____ Federal Open Market Committee
- _____ Federal funds
- _____ Federal funds rate
- _____ Open market
- _____ Rate
- _____ Recessionary gap
- _____ Taylor rule
- _____ Unemployment
- _____ Interest
- _____ Interest rate

14. Monetary Policy

CHAPTER OUTLINE: KEY TERMS, PEOPLE, PLACES, CONCEPTS

	Exchange
	Exchange rate
	Management
	Aggregate expenditure
	Investment
	Real interest rate
	Bank
	Consumption
	Loan
	Loanable funds
	Market
	Money market
	Recession
	Bank reserves
	Reserve
	Real GDP
	Gross domestic product
	Economy
	Financial crisis
	Capital
	Troubled Asset Relief Program

14. Monetary Policy
CHAPTER OUTLINE: KEY TERMS, PEOPLE, PLACES, CONCEPTS

	Economic recovery
	Congressional Budget Office

CHAPTER HIGHLIGHTS & NOTES: KEY TERMS, PEOPLE, PLACES, CONCEPTS

Federal Reserve	The Federal Reserve System (also known as the Federal Reserve, and informally as the Fed) is the central banking system of the United States. It was created on December 23, 1913, with the enactment of the Federal Reserve Act, largely in response to a series of financial panics, particularly a severe panic in 1907. Over time, the roles and responsibilities of the Federal Reserve System have expanded, and its structure has evolved. Events such as the Great Depression were major factors leading to changes in the system.
Federal Reserve Act	The Federal Reserve Act is an Act of Congress that created and set up the Federal Reserve System, the central banking system of the United States of America, and granted it the legal authority to issue Federal Reserve Notes, now commonly known as the U.S. Dollar, and Federal Reserve Bank Notes as legal tender. The Act was signed into law by President Woodrow Wilson.
Monetary policy	Monetary policy is the process by which the monetary authority of a country controls the supply of money, often targeting a rate of interest for the purpose of promoting economic growth and stability. The official goals usually include relatively stable prices and low unemployment. Monetary economics provides insight into how to craft optimal monetary policy.
Stability	In probability theory, the stability of a random variable is the property that a linear combination of two independent copies of the variable has the same distribution, up to location and scale parameters. The distributions of random variables having this property are said to be 'stable distributions'. Results available in probability theory show that all possible distributions having this property are members of a four-parameter family of distributions.
Bernanke	Ben Shalom Bernanke is an American economist at the Brookings Institution who served two terms as chairman of the Federal Reserve, the central bank of the United States from 2006 to 2014. During his tenure as chairman, Bernanke oversaw the Federal Reserve's response to the late-2000s financial crisis. Before becoming Federal Reserve chairman, Bernanke was a tenured professor at Princeton University and chaired the department of economics there from 1996 to September 2002, when he went on public service leave.

14. Monetary Policy

CHAPTER HIGHLIGHTS & NOTES: KEY TERMS, PEOPLE, PLACES, CONCEPTS

Consumer price index	A consumer price index measures changes in the price level of a market basket of consumer goods and services purchased by households. The Consumer price index in the United States is defined by the Bureau of Labor Statistics as 'a measure of the average change over time in the prices paid by urban consumers for a market basket of consumer goods and services.'
	The Consumer price index is a statistical estimate constructed using the prices of a sample of representative items whose prices are collected periodically. Sub-indexes and sub-sub-indexes are computed for different categories and sub-categories of goods and services, being combined to produce the overall index with weights reflecting their shares in the total of the consumer expenditures covered by the index.
Core inflation	Core inflation represents the long run trend in the price level. In measuring long run inflation, transitory price changes should be excluded. One way of accomplishing this is by excluding items frequently subject to volatile prices, like food and energy.
Inflationary gap	An inflationary gap, in economics, is the amount by which the actual gross domestic product exceeds potential full-employment GDP. It is one type of output gap, the other being a recessionary gap.
Output gap	The GDP gap or the output gap is the difference between actual GDP or actual output and potential GDP. The calculation for the output gap is Y-Y* where Y is actual output and Y* is potential output. If this calculation yields a positive number it is called an inflationary gap and indicates the growth of aggregate demand is outpacing the growth of aggregate supply--possibly creating inflation; if the calculation yields a negative number it is called a recessionary gap--possibly signifying deflation.
	The percentage GDP gap is the actual GDP minus the potential GDP divided by the potential GDP.
	$$\frac{(GDP_{actual} - GDP_{potential})}{GDP_{potential}}$$
Personal consumption	The Personal Consumption Expenditure measure is the component statistic for consumption in GDP collected by the BEA. It consists of the actual and imputed expenditures of households and includes data pertaining to durable and non-durable goods and services. It is essentially a measure of goods and services targeted towards individuals and consumed by individuals.
	The PCE price index (PCEPI), also referred to as the PCE deflator, PCE price deflator, or the Implicit Price Deflator for Personal Consumption Expenditures (IPD for PCE) by the BEA, and as the Chain-type Price Index for Personal Consumption Expenditures (CTPIPCE) by the FOMC, is a United States-wide indicator of the average increase in prices for all domestic personal consumption.

14. Monetary Policy

CHAPTER HIGHLIGHTS & NOTES: KEY TERMS, PEOPLE, PLACES, CONCEPTS

Operational	An operational definition is a result of the process of operationalization and is used to define something in terms of a process (or set of validation tests) needed to determine its existence, duration, and quantity. Since the degree of operationalization can vary itself, it can result in a more or less operational definition. The procedures included in definitions should be repeatable by anyone or at least by peers.
Federal Open Market Committee	The Federal Open Market Committee, a committee within the Federal Reserve System (the Fed), is charged under United States law with overseeing the nation's open market operations (i.e., the Fed's buying and selling of United States Treasury securities). It is this Federal Reserve committee which makes key decisions about interest rates and the growth of the United States money supply. It is the principal organ of United States national monetary policy.
Federal funds	In the United States, federal funds are overnight borrowings between banks and other entities to maintain their bank reserves at the Federal Reserve. Banks keep reserves at Federal Reserve Banks to meet their reserve requirements and to clear financial transactions. Transactions in the federal funds market enable depository institutions with reserve balances in excess of reserve requirements to lend reserves to institutions with reserve deficiencies.
Federal funds rate	In the United States, the federal funds rate is the interest rate at which depository institutions actively trade balances held at the Federal Reserve, called federal funds, with each other, usually overnight, on an uncollateralized basis. Institutions with surplus balances in their accounts lend those balances to institutions in need of larger balances. The federal funds rate is an important benchmark in financial markets.
Open market	The term open market is used generally to refer to a situation close to free trade and in a more specific technical sense to interbank trade in securities. In principle, a fully open market is a completely free market in which all economic actors can trade without any external constraint.
Rate	In mathematics, a rate is a ratio between two measurements with different units. If the unit or quantity in respect of which something is changing is not specified, usually the rate is per unit time. However, a rate of change can be specified per unit time, or per unit of length or mass or another quantity.
Recessionary gap	The GDP gap or the output gap is the difference between actual GDP or actual output and potential GDP. The calculation for the output gap is Y-Y* where Y is actual output and Y* is potential output. If this calculation yields a positive number it is called an inflationary gap and indicates the growth of aggregate demand is outpacing the growth of aggregate supply--possibly creating inflation; if the calculation yields a negative number it is called a recessionary gap--possibly signifying deflation. The percentage GDP gap is the actual GDP minus the potential GDP divided by the potential GDP.

14. Monetary Policy

CHAPTER HIGHLIGHTS & NOTES: KEY TERMS, PEOPLE, PLACES, CONCEPTS

	$(GDP_{actual} - GDP_{potential}) / GDP_{potential}$ {displaystyle {(GDP_{actual}-GDP_{potential})} over {GDP_{potential}}}.
Taylor rule	In economics, a Taylor rule is a monetary-policy rule that stipulates how much the central bank should change the nominal interest rate in response to changes in inflation, output, or other economic conditions. In particular, the rule stipulates that for each one-percent increase in inflation, the central bank should raise the nominal interest rate by more than one percentage point. This aspect of the rule is often called the Taylor principle.
Unemployment	Unemployment occurs when people are without work and actively seeking work. The unemployment rate is a measure of the prevalence of unemployment and it is calculated as a percentage by dividing the number of unemployed individuals by all individuals currently in the labor force. During periods of recession, an economy usually experiences a relatively high unemployment rate.
Interest	Interest is a fee paid by a borrower of assets to the owner as a form of compensation for the use of the assets. It is most commonly the price paid for the use of borrowed money, or money earned by deposited funds.

When money is borrowed, interest is typically paid to the lender as a percentage of the principal, the amount owed to the lender. |
Interest rate	An interest rate is the rate at which interest is paid by a borrower for the use of money that they borrow from a lender (creditor). Specifically, the interest rate is a percent of principal (P) paid a certain amount of times (m) per period (usually quoted per annum). For example, a small company borrows capital from a bank to buy new assets for its business, and in return the lender receives interest at a predetermined interest rate for deferring the use of funds and instead lending it to the borrower.
Exchange	An exchange, or bourse, is a highly organized market where tradable securities, commodities, foreign exchange, futures, and options contracts are sold and bought.
Exchange rate	In finance, an exchange rate between two currencies is the rate at which one currency will be exchanged for another. It is also regarded as the value of one country's currency in terms of another currency. For example, an interbank exchange rate of 91 Japanese yen (JPY, ¥) to the United States dollar (US$) means that ¥91 will be exchanged for each US$1 or that US$1 will be exchanged for each ¥91. Exchange rates are determined in the foreign exchange market, which is open to a wide range of different types of buyers and sellers where currency trading is continuous: 24 hours a day except weekends, i.e. trading from 20:15 GMT on Sunday until 22:00 GMT Friday.

14. Monetary Policy

CHAPTER HIGHLIGHTS & NOTES: KEY TERMS, PEOPLE, PLACES, CONCEPTS

Management	Management in businesses and other organizations, including not-for-profit organizations and government bodies, refers to the individuals who set the strategy of the organization and coordinate the efforts of employees to accomplish objectives by using available human, financial and other resources efficiently and effectively. Resourcing encompasses the deployment and manipulation of human resources, financial resources, technological resources, natural resources and other resources. Management is also an academic discipline, a social science whose objective is to study social organization and organizational leadership.
Aggregate expenditure	In economics, Aggregate Expenditure is a measure of national income. Aggregate Expenditure is defined as the current value of all the finished goods and services in the economy. The aggregate expenditure is thus the sum total of all the expenditures undertaken in the economy by the factors during a given time period.
Investment	Investment is time, energy, or matter spent in the hope of future benefits. Investment has different meanings in economics and finance. In economics, investment is the accumulation of newly produced physical entities, such as factories, machinery, houses, and goods inventories.
Real interest rate	The real interest rate is the rate of interest an investor expects to receive after allowing for inflation. It can be described more formally by the Fisher equation, which states that the real interest rate is approximately the nominal interest rate minus the inflation rate. If, for example, an investor were able to lock in a 5% interest rate for the coming year and anticipated a 2% rise in prices, they would expect to earn a real interest rate of 3%.
Bank	A bank is a financial institution and a financial intermediary that accepts deposits and channels those deposits into lending activities, either directly by loaning or indirectly through capital markets. A bank links together customers that have capital deficits and customers with capital surpluses. Due to their influential status within the financial system and upon national economies, banks are highly regulated in most countries.
Consumption	Consumption is a major concept in economics and is also studied by many other social sciences. Economists are particularly interested in the relationship between consumption and income, and therefore in economics the consumption function plays a major role. Different schools of economists define production and consumption differently.
Loan	An introductory rate is an interest rate charged to a customer during the initial stages of a loan.

14. Monetary Policy

CHAPTER HIGHLIGHTS & NOTES: KEY TERMS, PEOPLE, PLACES, CONCEPTS

	The rate, which can be as low as 0%, is not permanent and after it expires a normal or higher than normal rate will apply. The purpose of the introductory rate is to market the loan to customers and to seem attractive.
Loanable funds	In economics, the loanable funds market is a hypothetical market that brings savers and borrowers together, also bringing together the money available in commercial banks and lending institutions available for firms and households to finance expenditures, either investments or consumption. Savers supply the loanable funds; for instance, buying bonds will transfer their money to the institution issuing the bond, which can be a firm or government. In return, borrowers demand loanable funds; when an institution sells a bond, it is demanding loanable funds.
Market	A financial market is a market in which people and entities can trade financial securities, commodities, and other fungible items of value at low transaction costs and at prices that reflect supply and demand. Securities include stocks and bonds, and commodities include precious metals or agricultural goods. There are both general markets (where many commodities are traded) and specialized markets (where only one commodity is traded).
Money market	As money became a commodity, the money market became a component of the financial markets for assets involved in short-term borrowing, lending, buying and selling with original maturities of one year or less. Trading in the money markets is done over the counter and is wholesale. Various instruments exist, such as Treasury bills, commercial paper, bankers' acceptances, deposits, certificates of deposit, bills of exchange, repurchase agreements, federal funds, and short-lived mortgage-, and asset-backed securities.
Recession	In economics, a recession is a business cycle contraction. It is a general slowdown in economic activity. Macroeconomic indicators such as GDP (gross domestic product), investment spending, capacity utilization, household income, business profits, and inflation fall, while bankruptcies and the unemployment rate rise.
Bank reserves	Bank reserves or central bank reserves are banks' holdings of deposits in accounts with their central bank, plus currency that is physically held in the bank's vault (vault cash). The central banks of some nations set minimum reserve requirements, which require banks to hold deposits at the central bank equivalent to a specified percentage of their liabilities (such as customer deposits). Even when no reserve requirements are set, banks commonly wish to hold some reserves, called desired reserves, against unexpected events such as unusually large net withdrawals by customers or even bank runs.
Reserve	In financial accounting, the term reserve is most commonly used to describe any part of shareholders' equity, except for basic share capital.

14. Monetary Policy

CHAPTER HIGHLIGHTS & NOTES: KEY TERMS, PEOPLE, PLACES, CONCEPTS

	In nonprofit accounting, an 'operating reserve' is commonly used to refer to unrestricted cash on hand available to sustain an organization, and nonprofit boards usually specify a target of maintaining several months of operating cash or a percentage of their annual income, called an Operating Reserve Ratio.
	Sometimes, reserve is used in the sense of the term provision; such a use, however, is inconsistent with the terminology suggested by International Accounting Standards Board.
Real GDP	Real Gross Domestic Product (real GDP) is a macroeconomic measure of the value of economic output adjusted for price changes . This adjustment transforms the money-value measure, nominal GDP, into an index for quantity of total output. GDP is the sum of consumer Spending, Investment made by industry, Excess of Exports over Imports and Government Spending.
Gross domestic product	Gross domestic product is the market value of all officially recognized final goods and services produced within a country in a year, or other given period of time. gross domestic product per capita is often considered an indicator of a country's standard of living.
	gross domestic product per capita is not a measure of personal income .
Economy	An economy or economic system consists of the production, distribution or trade, and consumption of limited goods and services by different agents in a given geographical location. The economic agents can be individuals, businesses, organizations, or governments. Transactions occur when two parties agree to the value or price of the transacted good or service, commonly expressed in a certain currency.
Financial crisis	The term financial crisis is applied broadly to a variety of situations in which some financial assets suddenly lose a large part of their nominal value. In the 19th and early 20th centuries, many financial crises were associated with banking panics, and many recessions coincided with these panics. Other situations that are often called financial crises include stock market crashes and the bursting of other financial bubbles, currency crises, and sovereign defaults.
Capital	In economics, capital goods, real capital, or capital assets are already-produced durable goods or any non-financial asset that is used in production of goods or services.
	Capital goods are not significantly consumed in the production process though they may depreciate. How a capital good or is maintained or returned to its pre-production state varies with the type of capital involved.
Troubled Asset Relief Program	The Troubled Asset Relief Program is a program of the United States government to purchase assets and equity from financial institutions to strengthen its financial sector that was signed into law by U.S. President George W. Bush on October 3, 2008. It was a component of the government's measures in 2008 to address the subprime mortgage crisis.

14. Monetary Policy

CHAPTER HIGHLIGHTS & NOTES: KEY TERMS, PEOPLE, PLACES, CONCEPTS

	The Troubled Asset Relief Program program originally authorized expenditures of $700 billion. The Dodd-Frank Wall Street Reform and Consumer Protection Act reduced the amount authorized to $475 billion.
Economic recovery	An economic recovery is the phase of the business cycle following a recession, during which an economy regains and exceeds peak employment and output levels achieved prior to downturn. A recovery period is typically characterized by abnormally high levels of growth in real gross domestic product, employment, corporate profits, and other indicators.
Congressional Budget Office	The Congressional Budget Office is a federal agency within the legislative branch of the United States government that provides economic data to Congress. The Congressional Budget Office was created as a nonpartisan agency by the Congressional Budget and Impoundment Control Act of 1974.

CHAPTER QUIZ: KEY TERMS, PEOPLE, PLACES, CONCEPTS

1. _____ is the process by which the monetary authority of a country controls the supply of money, often targeting a rate of interest for the purpose of promoting economic growth and stability. The official goals usually include relatively stable prices and low unemployment. Monetary economics provides insight into how to craft optimal _____.

    a. Monetary policy
    b. Bank failure
    c. Jewish Social Democratic Party
    d. Bundism

2. A financial _____ is a _____ in which people and entities can trade financial securities, commodities, and other fungible items of value at low transaction costs and at prices that reflect supply and demand. Securities include stocks and bonds, and commodities include precious metals or agricultural goods.

    There are both general _____s (where many commodities are traded) and specialized _____s (where only one commodity is traded).

    a. Financial market
    b. Market
    c. Bank failure
    d. Bank code

3. . The _____ Expenditure measure is the component statistic for consumption in GDP collected by the BEA.

14. Monetary Policy

CHAPTER QUIZ: KEY TERMS, PEOPLE, PLACES, CONCEPTS

It consists of the actual and imputed expenditures of households and includes data pertaining to durable and non-durable goods and services. It is essentially a measure of goods and services targeted towards individuals and consumed by individuals.

The PCE price index (PCEPI), also referred to as the PCE deflator, PCE price deflator, or the Implicit Price Deflator for _____ Expenditures (IPD for PCE) by the BEA, and as the Chain-type Price Index for _____ Expenditures (CTPIPCE) by the FOMC, is a United States-wide indicator of the average increase in prices for all domestic _____.

   a. Christmas Price Index
   b. Personal consumption
   c. Higher Education Price Index
   d. Lipstick index

4. The _____ is an Act of Congress that created and set up the Federal Reserve System, the central banking system of the United States of America, and granted it the legal authority to issue Federal Reserve Notes, now commonly known as the U.S. Dollar, and Federal Reserve Bank Notes as legal tender. The Act was signed into law by President Woodrow Wilson.

   a. Bank Bill of 1791
   b. Federal Reserve Act
   c. Capital Access for Small Community Financial Institutions Act
   d. Check 21 Act

5. The _____ System (also known as the _____, and informally as the Fed) is the central banking system of the United States. It was created on December 23, 1913, with the enactment of the _____ Act, largely in response to a series of financial panics, particularly a severe panic in 1907. Over time, the roles and responsibilities of the _____ System have expanded, and its structure has evolved. Events such as the Great Depression were major factors leading to changes in the system.

   a. Gresham's Law
   b. Federal Reserve
   c. Nash equilibrium
   d. Federal Reserve

ANSWER KEY
14. Monetary Policy

1. a
2. b
3. b
4. b
5. d

You can take the complete Online Interactive Chapter Practice Test

for 14. Monetary Policy
on all key terms, persons, places, and concepts.

No Additional Costs

http://www.Cram101.com

Register, send an email request to Travis.Reese@Cram101.com to get your user Id and password.

Include your customer order number, and ISBN number from your studyguide Retailer.

15. International Trade Policy

CHAPTER OUTLINE: KEY TERMS, PEOPLE, PLACES, CONCEPTS

	Export
	Service
	Comparative advantage
	Consumer
	Gain
	Free trade
	Tariff
	General Agreement on Tariffs and Trade
	Revenue
	Import quota
	World Trade Organization
	North American Free Trade Agreement
	Subsidies
	Base period
	International trade
	Trade
	Infant industry
	Unemployment benefits
	Unemployment
	Bank
	Bank of America

15. International Trade Policy

CHAPTER OUTLINE: KEY TERMS, PEOPLE, PLACES, CONCEPTS

	Great Depression
	Monetarism
	Macroeconomics

CHAPTER HIGHLIGHTS & NOTES: KEY TERMS, PEOPLE, PLACES, CONCEPTS

Export	The term export means shipping the goods and services out of the port of a country. The seller of such goods and services is referred to as an 'exporter' who is based in the country of export whereas the overseas based buyer is referred to as an 'importer'. In International Trade, 'exports' refers to selling goods and services produced in the home country to other markets.
Service	In economics, a service is an intangible commodity. That is, services are an example of intangible economic goods. Service provision is often an economic activity where the buyer does not generally, except by exclusive contract, obtain exclusive ownership of the thing purchased.
Comparative advantage	In economics, comparative advantage refers to the ability of a party to produce a particular good or service at a lower marginal and opportunity cost over another. Even if one country is more efficient in the production of all goods (absolute advantage in all goods) than the other, both countries will still gain by trading with each other, as long as they have different relative efficiencies. For example, if, using machinery, a worker in one country can produce both shoes and shirts at 6 per hour, and a worker in a country with less machinery can produce either 2 shoes or 4 shirts in an hour, each country can gain from trade because their internal trade-offs between shoes and shirts are different.
Consumer	A consumer is a person or group of people, such as a household, who are the final users of products or services. The consumer's use is final in the sense that the product is usually not improved by the use.
Gain	In financial accounting, a gain is the increase in owner's equity resulting from something other than the day to day earnings from recurrent operations, and are not associated with investments or withdrawals.

15. International Trade Policy

CHAPTER HIGHLIGHTS & NOTES: KEY TERMS, PEOPLE, PLACES, CONCEPTS

Free trade	Free trade is a policy in international markets in which governments do not restrict imports or exports. Free trade is exemplified by the European Union / European Economic Area and the North American Free Trade Agreement, which have established open markets. Most nations are today members of the World Trade Organization (WTO) multilateral trade agreements.
Tariff	A tariff is a tax on imports or exports (an international trade tariff), or a list of prices for such things as rail service, bus routes, and electrical usage (electrical tariff, etc).. The meaning in (1) is now the more common meaning. The meaning in (2) is historically earlier.
General Agreement on Tariffs and Trade	The General Agreement on Tariffs and Trade was a multilateral agreement regulating international trade. According to its preamble, its purpose was the 'substantial reduction of tariffs and other trade barriers and the elimination of preferences, on a reciprocal and mutually advantageous basis.' It was negotiated during the United Nations Conference on Trade and Employment and was the outcome of the failure of negotiating governments to create the International Trade Organization (ITO). GATT was signed in 1947 and lasted until 1994, when it was replaced by the World Trade Organization in 1995.
Revenue	In business, revenue or turnover is income that a company receives from its normal business activities, usually from the sale of goods and services to customers. In many countries, revenue is referred to as turnover. Some companies receive revenue from interest, royalties, or other fees.
Import quota	An import quota is a limit on the quantity of a good that can be produced abroad and sold domestically. It is a type of protectionist trade restriction that sets a physical limit on the quantity of a good that can be imported into a country in a given period of time. If a quota is put on a good, less of it is imported.
World Trade Organization	The World Trade Organization is an organization that intends to supervise and liberalize international trade. The organization officially commenced on 1 January 1995 under the Marrakech Agreement, replacing the General Agreement on Tariffs and Trade (GATT), which commenced in 1948. The organization deals with regulation of trade between participating countries; it provides a framework for negotiating and formalizing trade agreements, and a dispute resolution process aimed at enforcing participant's adherence to World Trade Organization agreements, which are signed by representatives of member governments and ratified by their parliaments. Most of the issues that the World Trade Organization focuses on derive from previous trade negotiations, especially from the Uruguay Round (1986-1994).
North American Free Trade Agreement	The North American Free Trade Agreement is an agreement signed by Canada, Mexico, and the United States, creating a trilateral trade bloc in North America. The agreement came into force on January 1, 1994. It superseded the Canada-United States Free Trade Agreement between the U.S. and Canada.

15. International Trade Policy

CHAPTER HIGHLIGHTS & NOTES: KEY TERMS, PEOPLE, PLACES, CONCEPTS

	North American Free Trade Agreement has two supplements: the North American Agreement on Environmental Cooperation (NAAEC) and the North American Agreement on Labor Cooperation (NAALC).
Subsidies	A subsidy is a form of financial or in kind support extended to an economic sector generally with the aim of promoting economic and social policy. Although commonly extended from Government, the term subsidy can relate to any type of support - for example from NGOs or implicit subsidies. Subsidies come in various forms including: direct (cash grants, interest-free loans) and indirect (tax breaks, insurance, low-interest loans, depreciation write-offs, rent rebates).
Base period	In economics, a base period or reference period is a point in time used as a reference point for comparison with other periods. It is generally used as a benchmark for measuring financial or economic data. Base periods typically provide a point of reference for economic studies, consumer demand, and unemployment benefit claims.
International trade	International trade is the exchange of capital, goods, and services across international borders or territories. In most countries, such trade represents a significant share of gross domestic product (GDP). While international trade has been present throughout much of history, its economic, social, and political importance has been on the rise in recent centuries.
Trade	In finance, a trade is an exchange of a security for 'cash', typically a short-dated promise to pay in the currency of the country where the 'exchange' is located.
Infant industry	In economics, an infant industry is a new industry, which in its early stages experiences relative difficulty or is absolutely incapable in competing with established competitors abroad. Governments are sometimes urged to support the development of infant industries, protecting home industries in their early stages, usually through subsidies or tariffs. Subsidies may be indirect, as in when import duties are imposed or some prohibition against the import of a raw or finished material is imposed.
Unemployment benefits	Unemployment benefits are social welfare payments made by the state or other authorised bodies to unemployed people. Benefits may be based on a compulsory para-governmental insurance system. Depending on the jurisdiction and the status of the person, those sums may be small, covering only basic needs, or may compensate the lost time proportionally to the previous earned salary.
Unemployment	Unemployment occurs when people are without work and actively seeking work. The unemployment rate is a measure of the prevalence of unemployment and it is calculated as a percentage by dividing the number of unemployed individuals by all individuals currently in the labor force.

15. International Trade Policy

CHAPTER HIGHLIGHTS & NOTES: KEY TERMS, PEOPLE, PLACES, CONCEPTS

Bank	A bank is a financial institution and a financial intermediary that accepts deposits and channels those deposits into lending activities, either directly by loaning or indirectly through capital markets. A bank links together customers that have capital deficits and customers with capital surpluses. Due to their influential status within the financial system and upon national economies, banks are highly regulated in most countries.
Bank of America	The Bank of America Corporation is an American multinational banking and financial services corporation headquartered in Charlotte, North Carolina. It is the second largest bank holding company in the United States by assets. As of 2010, Bank of America is the fifth-largest company in the United States by total revenue, and the third-largest non-oil company in the U.S. (after Walmart and General Electric).
Great Depression	The Great Depression was a severe worldwide economic depression in the decade preceding World War II. The timing of the Great Depression varied across nations, but in most countries it started in 1930 and lasted until the late 1930s or middle 1940s. It was the longest, deepest, and most widespread depression of the 20th century. In the 21st century, the Great Depression is commonly used as an example of how far the world's economy can decline.
Monetarism	Monetarism is a school of economic thought that emphasizes the role of governments in controlling the amount of money in circulation. It is the view within monetary economics that variation in the money supply has major influences on national output in the short run and the price level over longer periods and that objectives of monetary policy are best met by targeting the growth rate of the money supply. Monetarism today is mainly associated with the work of Milton Friedman, who was among the generation of economists to accept Keynesian economics and then criticize Keynes' theory of gluts using fiscal policy (government spending).
Macroeconomics	Macroeconomics is a branch of economics dealing with the performance, structure, behavior, and decision-making of an economy as a whole, rather than individual markets. This includes national, regional, and global economies. With microeconomics, macroeconomics is one of the two most general fields in economics.

15. International Trade Policy

CHAPTER QUIZ: KEY TERMS, PEOPLE, PLACES, CONCEPTS

1. The _____ is an organization that intends to supervise and liberalize international trade. The organization officially commenced on 1 January 1995 under the Marrakech Agreement, replacing the General Agreement on Tariffs and Trade (GATT), which commenced in 1948. The organization deals with regulation of trade between participating countries; it provides a framework for negotiating and formalizing trade agreements, and a dispute resolution process aimed at enforcing participant's adherence to _____ agreements, which are signed by representatives of member governments and ratified by their parliaments. Most of the issues that the _____ focuses on derive from previous trade negotiations, especially from the Uruguay Round (1986-1994).

    a. World Trade Organization
    b. Caput Mundi
    c. Continental union
    d. Cosmopolitan democracy

2. _____ is a policy in international markets in which governments do not restrict imports or exports. _____ is exemplified by the European Union / European Economic Area and the North American _____ Agreement, which have established open markets. Most nations are today members of the World Trade Organization (WTO) multilateral trade agreements.

    a. Customs territory
    b. Free trade zone
    c. Free trade
    d. Technical barriers to trade

3. The term _____ means shipping the goods and services out of the port of a country. The seller of such goods and services is referred to as an 'exporter' who is based in the country of _____ whereas the overseas based buyer is referred to as an 'importer'. In International Trade, '_____s' refers to selling goods and services produced in the home country to other markets.

    a. Endangered Species Act
    b. Energy Task Force
    c. Anglo Irish Bank Corporation Act 2009
    d. Export

4. In economics, a _____ is an intangible commodity. That is, _____s are an example of intangible economic goods.

    _____ provision is often an economic activity where the buyer does not generally, except by exclusive contract, obtain exclusive ownership of the thing purchased.

    a. Base period
    b. Benefit incidence
    c. Blanket order
    d. Service

15. International Trade Policy

CHAPTER QUIZ: KEY TERMS, PEOPLE, PLACES, CONCEPTS

5. The _____ was a multilateral agreement regulating international trade. According to its preamble, its purpose was the 'substantial reduction of tariffs and other trade barriers and the elimination of preferences, on a reciprocal and mutually advantageous basis.' It was negotiated during the United Nations Conference on Trade and Employment and was the outcome of the failure of negotiating governments to create the International Trade Organization (ITO). GATT was signed in 1947 and lasted until 1994, when it was replaced by the World Trade Organization in 1995.

    a. Gresham's Law
    b. Canada Corn Act
    c. General Agreement on Tariffs and Trade
    d. Court of Exchequer

ANSWER KEY
15. International Trade Policy

1. a
2. c
3. d
4. d
5. c

You can take the complete Online Interactive Chapter Practice Test

for 15. International Trade Policy
on all key terms, persons, places, and concepts.

No Additional Costs

http://www.Cram101.com

Register, send an email request to Travis.Reese@Cram101.com to get your user Id and password.

Include your customer order number, and ISBN number from your studyguide Retailer.

Other Facts101 e-Books and Tests

Want More?
JustTheFacts101.com...

Jtf101.com provides the outlines and highlights of your textbooks, just like this e-StudyGuide, but also gives you the PRACTICE TESTS, and other exclusive study tools for all of your textbooks.

Learn More. *Just click*
http://www.JustTheFacts101.com/

CPSIA information can be obtained
at www.ICGtesting.com
Printed in the USA
LVHW05s0133150618
580837LV00002B/180/P